# The Voluntary Sector, the State and Social Work in Britain

# The Voluntary Sector, the State and Social Work in Britain

The Charity Organisation Society/Family Welfare Association since 1869

Jane Lewis

*Professor of Social Policy*
*London School of Economics and Political Science*

Edward Elgar

Published by
Edward Elgar Publishing Limited
Gower House
Croft Road
Aldershot
Hants GU11 3HR
England

Edward Elgar Publishing Company
Old Post Road
Brookfield
Vermont 05036
USA


**British Library Cataloguing in Publication Data**
Voluntary Sector, the State and Social
Work in Britain:Charity Organisation
Society/Family Welfare Association Since
1869
  I. Lewis, Jane
  361.370941

**Library of Congress Cataloguing in Publication Data**
Lewis, Jane (Jane E.)
    The voluntary sector, the state, and social work in Britain : the
  Charity Organisation Society/Family Welfare Association since 1869 /
  Jane Lewis.
      p.   cm.
    Includes bibliographical references.
    1. Charity Organisation Society (London, England)—History.
  2. Family Welfare Association (Great Britain)—History.   3. Social
  service—Great Britain—History.    4. Charities—Great Britain—
  History.   I. Family Welfare Association (Great Britain)
  II. Title.
  HV250.L8L49 1995
  361.8'0941—dc20                                                      94–31726
                                                                          CIP

ISBN 1 85898 188 3

Printed in Great Britain by Ipswich Book Co. Ltd., Ipswich, Suffolk.

# Contents

# Preface

This book was written in the Family Welfare Association's 125th year, but it is not intended as an institutional history of the organisation. Rather, the long history of the FWA, which began life as the Charity Organisation Society, is used as a means of saying something about two main issues: the changing nature of relationships between voluntary organisations and the state, and the history of social work. The focus is thus very much on the relationship between the FWA and its external environment.

I am grateful to those members and former members of the Association who helped me think through aspects of these issues and who also permitted me to borrow their personal papers relating to the FWA for the period 1960–90, for which documentation is scarce. Lynne Berry, Rose Mary Braithwaite, Anne Dickinson, Enid Levin, Helen and Roger Martyn and Bob Pinker were kind enough to comment on the manuscript.

JANE LEWIS

# Introduction: the COS, the FWA and the mixed economy of welfare

## I

The founders of the Charity Organisation Society believed that it was not necessary or desirable for the state to extend its involvement in social welfare provision. Not only was the voluntary sector believed to be equal to the task, but reliance on the principle of 'true charity' would also ensure social progress. The COS is worth exploring in terms of its ideas as well as its practice because it focused and openly discussed so many of the dilemmas of the late Victorian period, dilemmas that still have purchase. COS leaders interrogated themselves and each other as to whether the tenets of classical political economy could be reconciled with the Christian injunction to give; as to the relative importance of economics and morals, and character and circumstance; and as to whether men were motivated more by altruism or by selfishness. They did not shy away from the big questions and were not afraid to form a view on them.

Certainly voluntary endeavour in nineteenth-century Britain was impressive in terms of both its range and size. Perhaps the best way of measuring the extent of charity is by the amount of money that was funnelled through it, although this is an extremely difficult task. As late as 1911 the gross annual receipts of registered charities exceeded public expenditure on the poor law and this sum excluded the money tied up in mutual aid, as well as in unregistered charities (Harris, 1990). While social spending on the part of the state rapidly outstripped private benevolence in the twentieth-century, Constance Braithwaite's 1938 study showed no slackening in the flow of contributions to the voluntary sector during the inter-war period. The provision of welfare in Britain has always been mixed, and the part played by the voluntary sector during the late nineteenth and early twentieth centuries was particularly important.

Yet the historiography of the British welfare state has tended to focus almost exclusively on the role of the state and to stress the eventual triumph of collectivism over individualism, with Britain emerging from the darkness of the poor law into the light of the Beveridge Plan of 1942 and the post-war welfare state. It is a story of linear development and progress. However, this story has been thrown into question by the apparent reversal of the late 1970s, which began with James Callaghan's (the Labour prime minister) speech of 1976 in which he told the Labour Party's Conference that governments could no longer expect to spend their way out of recessions, and continued with Margaret Thatcher, who sought to diminish the role of the state in terms of both public expenditure and size of bureaucracy, and to promote the market, the voluntary sector and the family as providers of welfare.

The profound nature of the shift is captured by the way in which Britain's place in the various typologies of welfare states that have been developed in the post-war period has changed. In the 1960s, Richard Titmuss suggested a threefold division: the institutional redistributive model, with universal access and citizenship-based entitlements to state welfare which characterised the Scandinavian countries and Britain; the industrial achievement performance model, based on insurance and tied to occupation, which was typical of continental European countries; and the residual model in which state welfare was means-tested and intended to be a matter of last resort, as was the case in the USA (Titmuss, 1974). In 1990, Gösta Esping Andersen provided a much more elaborate classification of welfare 'regimes' – regime because he looked at the interaction between work and welfare – based on a 'decommodification index', meaning the extent to which the state will support male workers who are out of the labour market for whatever reason (Esping Andersen, 1990). Esping Andersen came up with 'three worlds of welfare', the social democratic, the catholic/conservative and the liberal. Roughly speaking, the same countries found their way into the equivalent categories – for example, the USA was residual in Titmuss's scheme and liberal in Esping Andersen's – but Britain moved from Titmuss's institutional redistributive category, which it shared with Sweden, to Esping Andersen's liberal category, alongside the USA.

These typologies are hardly robust and it is possible to challenge them from a variety of angles. They deal only with the state provision of welfare and, as Kuhnle and Selle (1992) have observed, if the voluntary sector is injected into Esping Andersen's typology, then any idea of a Scandinavian model disappears. Denmark, Norway and Sweden have had very different patterns of voluntary organisation.[1] But the typologies are nonetheless suggestive. Certainly British historians have begun to rethink the periodisation of the modern welfare state and to ask whether the period of what is coming to be called the 'classic welfare state' (from 1945 to 1976) (Digby, 1989; Lowe, 1993) should be seen as exceptional rather than some sort of culmination. More fundamentally still, it has become necessary to rethink the *nature* of the welfare state.

Rather than seeing the story of the modern welfare state as a simple movement from individualism to collectivism and ever-increasing amounts of (benevolent) state intervention, it is more accurate to see Britain as always having had a mixed economy of welfare, in which the state, the voluntary sector, the family and the market have played different parts at different points in time. This might have been more obvious earlier had British historians and social policy analysts engaged in more European comparative research. For example, many European countries have had long experience of the kind of separation of (state) finance from (private and voluntary) provision in the realm of social services, something that has become an explicit policy goal in respect of British social services since 1988. In a majority of continental European countries a mixed economy, or welfare pluralism, has been the norm.

There is a growing, mainly American, literature which seeks to explain the existence of voluntary organisations and the role they play in social provision. Economists argue that they are the result of state or market failure. For example, Hansmann (1987) has suggested that, where information asymmetries exist, contract failure occurs. Contract mechanisms may fail to provide consumers with the adequate means to police producers, and where consumers cannot evaluate services and need protection by providers non-profit organisations will appear more trustworthy. Weisbrod (1988) has stressed the extent to which the market or the state may fail to meet minority demands, which will then be met by voluntary organisations, but as the demand expands it will likely be met by the state. This kind of explanation tends to put the state, the market and the voluntary sector in separate boxes, such that the relationship between the state and the voluntary sector in particular becomes at best complementary and often conflictual. There is little room for the kind of conceptualisation of voluntary organisations as part and parcel of the fabric of the state that was the hallmark of nineteenth-century Britain and also seems to have characterised the Norwegian experience (Kuhnle and Selle, 1992).

Salamon's (1987, 1990) theory of voluntary sector failure is more broadly in tune with the historical evidence. He has argued that voluntary organisations were perceived in most western countries as the first line of defence, but their weaknesses – insufficiency, particularism, paternalism and amateurism – rendered increasing cooperation with the state inevitable. Interestingly, some of the founders of the Charity Organisation Society also propounded a theory of voluntary failure to explain the existence of the poor law. What is important about Salamon's theory is not so much the extent to which it fits the empirical evidence. The voluntary sector is so diverse and differs so greatly in its historical development between countries that it is highly unlikely that such single-discipline theories using a relatively small range of variables could be successfully applied to all cases. Thus, while Hansmann's notion of contract failure fits the experience of US savings banks rather well, it has little to offer the cases of social service provision in health, child welfare, education or housing in the USA where different forms of voluntary/statutory cooperation seem to have prevailed (Gronjberg, 1987). Nor is it sufficient to explain why the provision of lifeboat services remains voluntary in Britain, but is a local government responsibility in Sweden, while the reverse is true of rural fire services. But Salamon is right to stress the error of compartmentalising voluntary, statutory and market provision. He prefers to look for the degree to which the boundaries between the sectors were in fact blurred. This is useful for the British case from the end of the nineteenth century, when the strict division between state provision, in the form of the poor law, and the market was significantly diminished, and when new forms of cooperation between the state and the voluntary sector, particularly in relation to government funding of voluntary organisations, became more common. But even this does not quite capture the complexity of the historical relationships, as Ware (1989) has recognised. Late nineteenth-century charity leaders advocated close cooperation with the poor law while at the same time insisting on a separate sphere for charity. The point is that both the conceptualisation and the nature of the late nineteenth-century state were quite different from those of the late twentieth. Thus the meaning of a call for greater reliance on voluntary provision in the 1980s and 1990s will be different from a similar set of convictions in the 1870s and 1880s.

## II

Nineteenth-century voluntary endeavour encompassed charity in the form of the better off assisting those who were less well off in a wide variety of ways; mutual aid, most importantly in the form of trade unions and friendly societies; and the informal help that the poor rendered the poor. The terms 'charity' and 'philanthropy' were often used interchangeably during the period to cover all or part of this endeavour.[2] There is plenty of evidence that late Victorian middle-class households made substantial contributions to charity; in the 1890s, it has been estimated that on average they spent a larger share of their income on charity than on any item in their budget except food (Prochaska, 1988). Nor was charitable giving confined to the middle class. A French study of the 1870s calculated that a large majority of British adults belonged to an average of between five or six voluntary organisations, which included trade unions and friendly societies, both of which played a major role in securing for their members financial protection against sickness and unemployment; savings societies of various kinds; and literary and scientific institutes (Harris, 1993). Frank Prochaska (1988) has also emphasised the extent to which the poor relied on the generosity of the poor in times of need, most of it organised informally. However, it is difficult to calculate the amount of money given by charities in poor relief. Humphreys (1991) has suggested that the medical charities and philanthropic public works accounted for a substantial part of Victorian voluntary endeavour and has argued that any claim that charity provided considerably more in poor relief than the poor law must be treated with suspicion. Still, it is impossible to deny that the voluntary sector bulked large in nineteenth-century social provision.

Charity was also exceedingly diverse. There were city missions; district visiting societies; mothers' meetings; a huge variety of provident clubs allowing working people to save for items such as the Christmas goose and boots, an expenditure which always posed a threat to the fragile family economy; organisations to meet almost any conceivable human (and animal) need, whether medical, financial or for leisure. In the 1870s, there were no fewer than five charities established with the aim of relieving Sunday gloom (Prochaska, 1988). Charity was inevitably patchy, a criticism that gathered force at the turn of the century, yet the numbers of ordinary people who would have had some contact with some form of organised charity were impressive. To take one of the lesser known forms, the mothers' meeting (which combined needlework and religion): Prochaska has estimated that some one million Edwardian women participated in these out of the 12 million who would have been of an age to attend. Within the compass of charitable effort, charity *organisation* comprised but a very small part. It was in part the number of potentially overlapping charities that made the founders of the Charity Organisation Society want to bring some order into the world of philanthropy.

How should we understand the size and variety of the nineteenth-century voluntary sector? In the first place it is worth reiterating the extent to which charitable effort was not just a 'top-down' affair. Yeo (1976) has shown how late nineteenth-century Reading had thriving working-class voluntary organisations as well as middle-class philanthropy and has suggested that at the end of the 1890s:

> The situation was fascinatingly poised. Landed or manufacturing philanthropy was insufficient. The state had not yet moved in. Professionals were not yet in complete control. There was thus space for other paths to be taken, including ones which quickly petered out or were blocked, but which at the time seemed possible carriers of working class ideas and organisation. (p. 216)

Yeo's picture of a strong set of community associations, generated by faith in localism and personally generated solutions in which the whole town took pride, is compelling. As was commonly the case outside London, especially in the north of England, the Charity Organisation Society was not central.

The motives of those involved in voluntary organisations were nevertheless diverse. While working people were in large measure prompted to engage in mutual aid or informal giving out of a very real fear of the want that even a short period of interrupted earnings could bring, the motives of the better off were more varied. Middle-class benevolence was to some extent due to a desire for status – to be listed as a subscriber to a voluntary hospital or other prominent charity carried some weight in the community – or to a desire not just to save the souls of others but to store up credit for one's own soul (Harrison, 1982). (Three-quarters of the charities established in the second half of the nineteenth-century were evangelical.) To the large numbers of middle-class women who joined voluntary organisations, such as parish visiting societies or indeed charity organisation societies, and who became visitors of the poor, charitable work represented one of the very few bridges to the world beyond the home and family. For many of these women visiting the poor was something of an adventure as well as a duty (Vicinus, 1985).

While there was, then, considerable self-interest behind middle-class benevolence, the prevailing commitment to altruism was probably a more important factor explaining the pull of charitable giving and voluntary work. Collini (1991) has suggested that, because altruistic aims were assumed to motivate, Victorians found social work an anti-dote to religious doubt. As he has further observed, there existed a hegemonic set of assumptions regarding 'the ideal of service, the duty to contribute to the common good, the need to make the best of oneself, the duty of self development and so on' (Collini, 1979, p. 49). The sincere search for 'right action' and 'right feeling', as Octavia Hill, the pioneer housing manager and member of the Charity Organisation Society, put it, was widespread. Classical political economists, who condemned unproductive expenditure in the form of charitable giving to the poor, and those who, like Beatrice Webb, turned away from an emphasis on the individual towards studying the problem of poverty through the methods of the social survey, often expressed their con-tempt of philanthropy by attaching to it the adjective 'sentimental'. However, the belief in charity was much more complicated than that. To those who became leaders of the Charity Organisation Society and spokesmen for charity more generally, such as C.S. Loch and Bernard Bosanquet, it amounted to a social principle. Charitable endeavour represented citizens united by moral purpose, voluntarily fulfilling their duty to those less fortunate than themselves. E.J. Urwick, who became the director of the COS's School of Sociology in 1903, spoke of a society in which true citizenship meant that 'we must feel the claims of fellow citizens' (Urwick, 1912, p. 194). Women were believed to have more purchase on feeling than men because of their maternal role, although this in turn meant that service to family would occupy a greater place in women's lives than in those of men. True feeling inspired forgetfulness of self and service to others, and true feeling could only be a product of a careful search of conscience which in turn depended on the development of character. The injunction to behave charitably thus amounted to a particular vision of an ethical society in which citizens motivated by altruism performed their duties towards one another voluntarily. The larger aims of and motives for charity are important because they explain the tenacity with which the COS de-fended its position, but they do not necessarily reflect what actually happened in practice. It was not for nothing that elderly people in the late twentieth-century remembered with bitterness having 'washed the charity' out of a garment, or that the COS itself acquired the label 'cringe or starve'. There was, in other words, a considerable gap between high flown ideals of charity as a social principle and charitable practice.

However, the way in which the place of charity was conceptualised means that it is mistaken to describe the nineteenth-century voluntary sector as something as big as or larger than statutory provision and as a wholly separate element from the state. This depiction consciously or unconsciously draws on the current conceptualisation of the voluntary sector as an *alternative* to the state and applies it to an earlier period. It is more accurate to see voluntary organisations in the late nineteenth-century as part of the way in which political leaders conceptualised the state. José Harris (1990, p. 67) has described the aim of Victorian governments as being 'to provide a framework of rules and guidelines designed to enable society very largely to run itself'. This did not amount to rank atomistic individualism: 'the corporate life of society was seen as expressed through voluntary associations and the local community, rather than through the persona of the state' (ibid.). Nineteenth-century Britain had effective central government institutions, but a small central bureaucracy and a strong desire to limit the activities of central government. Voluntary organisations may best be conceptualised as part of a range of 'buffer institutions' (Thane, 1990, p. 1) that developed between the central state and the citizen and which were conceived of as being part of the fabric of the state. They were not, as Pat Thane (1993, p. 358) has remarked, 'the fortuitous corollary of the limited state but [were] integral to the conceptualization of that state by its leaders'.

In the nineteenth and early twentieth centuries, much state social provision was locally financed and locally administered. For example, the poor law was controlled by locally elected boards of guardians from 1834 and education by locally elected school boards from 1870. It was only from the end of the nineteenth-century that matters of social policy gradually became the stuff of 'high politics' (Harris, 1993), prompted in large part by the rapid increase in the financial burden experienced at the local level. Rates in London rose between 30 and 50 per cent in the period 1891–1906. Thus the welfare reforms of the Liberal government of 1906–14 relied on a quite different pattern of finance: taxation in the case of old age pensions and insurance against sickness and unemployment (which also required a state contribution out of taxation). However, in respect of its administration, national insurance in particular represented an attempt to reconcile state compulsion with mutual aid voluntarism; trade unions and friendly societies were invited to administer the policy.

The fact that social provision was local made it easier for a measure of welfare pluralism to exist. As the role of central government in social provision grew, so the balance between the voluntary and the statutory sector shifted. During the 1980s and 1990s, the New Right has hankered after 'little battalions' (Willetts, 1992); that is, social provision determined by community and neighbourhood. However, such an idea was arguably more feasible in the late nineteenth-century when the central state left local territory relatively free from control.

The circumstances of the founding of the Charity Organisation Society in 1869 provide a good illustration of the nature of the relationship between the statutory and the voluntary sectors in this period. From the beginning, the COS's sphere of action was defined in relation to the poor law. The Goschen Minute on the Relief to the Poor in the Metropolis, issued by the central Poor Law Board in 1870 (C.123), set out the relationship between the poor law and voluntary action and was welcomed by the members of the Council of the London COS as being in complete harmony with their approach. George G. Goschen stated his concern about the rise in pauperism (destitution, and as such distinct from poverty) and the effect it might have on the public, increasing their anxiety and their indiscriminate giving. In face of this possibility, he was anxious to promote an agreed set of limits on charitable and poor law relief. Goschen's main concern was to hold the line on poor law relief. The role he set out for charity was to assist those on the verge of destitution, in other words to prevent them becoming a public charge, while the state was conceptualised as a provider of last resort. Sidney and Beatrice Webb (1912, p. 229) referred to this as the 'cowcatcher' theory of charitable action. Goschen thus advocated cooperation between the statutory and voluntary sectors on similar tasks, while maintaining separate spheres of action. The COS eagerly set out to cooperate at the local level with boards of guardians in order to prevent pauperism.

The COS was concerned first and foremost about extreme poverty. It was distinctive in that its leaders attempted to set out in some detail their ideas about poverty and pauperism and the role that the state and the voluntary sector should play in poor relief. The COS accepted the doctrine of the 1834 Poor Law Amendment Act, which erected a firm boundary between the state and the market. The first half of the twentieth century saw particular groups – the elderly, skilled workers and to some extent children – being taken outside the ambit of the poor law and made eligible for old age pensions, national health and unemployment insurance, and school meals and medical inspection, respectively. But the poor law was not finally abolished until 1948. Anyone declaring himself in need of relief by the poor law authorities had to prove himself to be genuinely destitute by being prepared to submit to the workhouse test. The aim of the Act was to abolish 'outdoor relief' (relief in money or kind given to people in their own homes) which, it was believed, could only serve further to sap the incentive to self-maintenance, and to force the destitute into the workhouse. Once there, they would be put to work at an unpleasant task, such as stone crushing in the case of men and oakum picking in the case of women, for which they would be paid at below market rates. Until 1885, anyone seeking medical relief under the poor law was also deprived of a vote (in the unlikely event that they had qualified for one under the limited franchise that then operated). The implementation of the Act was never this rigorous. Outdoor relief was never abolished and conditions in workhouses varied widely from place to place. However, the basic idea of segregating paupers from market and civil society was important and was fundamentally different from twentieth-century ideas about income maintenance in modern welfare states, which ceased to operate on a principle of strict deterrence and aimed to reintegrate recipients of benefit into the workforce as quickly as possible. Ware and Goodin (1990) have contrasted the poor law's residualist, needs-led model of relief, in which everyone was entitled to aid but at the price of sundering contact with the wider world, with later insurance, contractually based models on the one hand, and social citizenship, rights-based models of welfare on the other.

The poor law model necessarily assumed that the destitute were responsible for their own fate. The thinking behind the Act of 1834 did not consider the possibility of social causes of pauperism. Yet while the Goschen Circular of 1870 urged boards of guardians to return to the principles of 1834 and relieve the able-bodied pauper only in a workhouse, it nevertheless also advised guardians to discriminate between the reputable and disreputable. As José Harris (1993, p. 238) has remarked, this admitted the idea that there might be social causes of pauperism which ticked away as 'a time bomb' in the poor law. The COS endorsed the view that pauperism was a moral condition, but also rapidly came to the conclusion that the 'deserving' had to be separated from the 'undeserving' and that charity could only hope to prevent people in the former category from becoming a public charge. However, the difficulty in drawing a firm line between the deserving and the undeserving – between those whose destitution was not due to personal failings such as drunkenness, but owed more to misfortune, such as an extended period of illness, and those who were hopelessly feckless and immoral – proved a continuing and central problem for the COS.

The objects of the COS were to improve the condition of the poor by cooperating with the poor law, to repress mendicity, to investigate and effectively assist the deserving and to promote good habits. Above all, the aim of the COS was to restore the deserving to 'self-maintenance', so that they became capable of engaging in market exchange and participating fully in civil society; the leaders of the COS often spoke of restoring people to full citizenship. Their aim was not then simply economic, but was related to their ideas about charity as a means of creating an ethical society. The key to the creation of such a society was character, which was the source of altruistic behaviour in the rich as much as self-supporting behaviour in the poor. The COS wanted to build up the character of those individuals and families who approached them for help. Visitors, or social workers as they became called, would work with families to help them back to self-maintenance. This might involve giving them financial help, but it was also likely to involve changing habits and attitudes towards work on the part of the male breadwinner, and towards housekeeping and childcare on the part of the wife and mother. Social work thus became the vehicle for implementing COS ideas and acquired a concomitant importance. Work with individuals was believed to be the way to achieve social change and the COS pioneered the training of its volunteer social workers.

The verdict on the COS during its most influential period, 1870–1909, has been mixed. In the minds of contemporaries and of historians since, the COS has been irreparably associated with the repression of mendicity and the abolition of all forms of doles and out-relief to the poor. Indeed, scientific charity has been broadly equated with the doctrines of the classical economists, who believed that any relief given to the poor without fully testing whether the applicant was truly destitute would only serve to increase the evil of pauperism (Fido, 1977). In her centennial history of the COS, Madeleine Rooff (1972) accepted that this accurately described the ideology of the organisation, but she attempted to distinguish it from what she perceived as the COS's

progressive ideas about social work practice. However, Gareth Stedman
Jones (1976) has argued strongly that it is impossible to separate theory
from practice; they must stand or fall together. From his study of
provincial charity organisation societies, Robert Humphreys (1991) has
concluded that the COS was populated by sincere, but inflexible, zeal-
ots who could not shake off their belief that the poor were inherently
lazy, but Vincent's (1984) study of COS theory has concluded that it
was by no means as crudely reactionary as this.

Even if Vincent is correct, and there is much evidence to support him
from the work of the younger leaders of the London Society, it may still
be, as David Owen (1965, p. 236) contended in his study of English
philanthropy, that COS ideas were 'rather preposterous'. Nevertheless,
it was in large part their ideas that gave the leaders of the COS such
public influence. For even though historians can rightly play down the
role of the COS in the wider world of philanthropy (Humphreys, 1991;
Prochaska, 1988), it is impossible to ignore its presence in the policy-
making arena. Commenting on the lack of opposition to the number of
COS representatives on the 1905–9 Royal Commission on the Poor
Laws, A.M. McBriar (1987, p. 194) observed that this was 'a sign of
wide acceptance of basic COS views in informed circles in Edwardian
times; indeed, it is probable that those views were widely accepted
without being thought of as being the peculiar property of the COS –
they were thought to be "common-sense"'. Thus, while the COS was
by no means the sole spokesman for the voluntary sector in the period
before the First World War, it was nonetheless a very important
'weathervane of opinion' (Finlayson, 1990, pp. 199–200).


# III

When the COS was founded, government and the leaders of the Society
had a common understanding of the role of charity and of the state in
regard to the problem of poverty and pauperism. To this extent, a form
of partnership may be said to have existed, albeit that its character was
very different from the partnership between the statutory and voluntary
sectors that began to be talked about in the inter-war years and fully to
emerge after World War II. For, while the COS held on firmly to its
views about the relative importance of charitable as opposed to statutory social provision, the balance between the two sectors was nevertheless shifting during the Edwardian period. When inter-war leaders of

the COS looked back they tended to catalogue a series of defeats for the ideas of the Society, particularly at the hands of the reforming Liberal government of 1906–14.

In 1920, Clement Attlee declared the poor law to be 'under sentence of death' largely because of the impossibility of determining whether someone was poor through his own fault (Attlee, 1920, p. 82). While Attlee was hardly an impartial observer, both his views on the poor law and his ringing indictment of the COS as its misguided partner were widely shared for different reasons by people across the political spectrum. The Liberal welfare reforms, particularly in the field of pensions and social insurance, both gave a greater role to the state in social provision and made it more a matter for central government than for local bodies. The reasons for this change in the balance between the voluntary and statutory sectors and in the very nature of the state are highly complex. Historians have called attention to a wide variety of factors: pragmatic financial issues, such as the increasing burden social provision placed on the local rates; bureaucratic developments involving the growth in the number of specialised central government departments and in their capacity for directing policy; Britain's changing economic position in a world of increased industrial competition, which resulted in both a squeeze on labour – elderly and less efficient workers, for example, became more vulnerable in the labour market – and social policies, such as pensions, to ameliorate the position of labour; changes in the content of liberalism, such that it stressed 'positive' rather than 'negative' liberty; and changing perceptions of social problems and their cause, particularly poverty.

Social investigators, such as Beatrice Webb, who worked on Charles Booth's survey of London during the 1880s, settlement house workers, such as Samuel Barnett, who founded Toynbee Hall, and a new generation of economists all questioned the basis of the principles of the 1834 Poor Law Amendment Act and of the role of charity as propounded by the COS. Beatrice Webb came to think that the COS's individual, face-to-face approach to the problem of poverty was hopeless, given the extent of the problem that was revealed by late nineteenth-century social investigation. Charles Booth himself remained an adherent of COS doctrines so far as the moral failure of the able-bodied went, but the evidence his survey provided of poverty in old age made him a convert to the idea of old age pensions. People like Barnett and the economist, Alfred Marshall, were concerned more about poverty than pauperism and were able to justify a greater role for the state in tackling it, urging voluntary organisations like the COS to cooperate with the state in such an endeavour. Edwardian advocates of 'national efficiency' developed this theme, suggesting that it was ridiculous for the great reforming power of the state to be withheld from all but the lunatic, the criminal and the pauper. It is notable that criticism of the poor law was usually accompanied by criticism of the COS because of the close relationship between them, and that critics came increasingly both from outside the Society and from within.

Increased state intervention in the social field has been interpreted as a response to pressure from below (echoing Sidney Webb's view that social reform was the obverse of franchise reform) on the one hand, and as an effort on the part of government to shore up free-market capitalism on the other. Such 'either/ors' tend to gloss over the contradictions. José Harris (1993, p. 218) has argued convincingly that 'the practical process by which change occurred was a piecemeal and unsystematic one, involving many ambiguities and inconsistencies in public policy and many attempts to harness together and reconcile social principles that were seemingly in tension'. A piece of legislation like national insurance, for example, sought to reconcile market forces with bureaucratic rationality and voluntarism. Indeed, there is little evidence that the early twentieth-century state set out to erode voluntarism in particular. Nevertheless, as William Beveridge (1948) recognised, compulsory social insurance sounded the death knell for mutual aid friendly societies, and Prochaska (1988) has suggested that the growth of government responsibility for welfare contributed to the devitalisation of Christian charity (although it is worth remembering the evidence provided by Constance Braithwaite (1938) at the end of the inter-war period which showed that charitable contributions in London had not declined). Against these pessimistic views of the effect of state intervention on charity must be set the argument that it was not so much government activity as the development of market society that served to erode altruism (Ware, 1990). In so far as the market expanded social relations beyond local communities and thus threatened the web of charitable relationships and autonomous organisations that had characterised the Victorian state, this argument carries weight. And, in an increasingly secular society, the moral imperative to altruistic behaviour retreated before the market's demand that individuals be self-interested.

Government intervention measured by public expenditure continued to grow rapidly during the inter-war years, although many forces within government, notably in the Treasury and the Government Actuary's Department, wished to see retreat. The COS alternated between holding up the Drage Return, which catalogued annual social services expenditure, as evidence of the ever-increasing evil of state intervention, and seeing in the seemingly endless manoeuvring of governments over eligibility criteria for social insurance and public assistance some, to its way of thinking, hopeful signs of the end of collectivism. The COS persisted in the view of statutory/voluntary relationships which it had held to from its founding and seized eagerly on the analysis of Mary Follett (1918), an American, who used the new psychology to argue for a rejection of ballot box democracy and party organisation in favour of voluntary neighbourhood organisation. This was merely to dress up old COS beliefs in new (psychological) clothes.

However, in practice the relationship between the state and the voluntary sector was changing. Prochaska (1988) has emphasised the extent to which voluntary agencies retained their autonomy during the inter-war years, but contemporaries stressed the financial difficulties of many voluntary organisations (not least the voluntary hospitals) and state subsidy to the voluntary sector increased. It was part of the rethinking of the relationship between the sectors that many people no longer viewed financial dependence on the state as problematic. In the years immediately before World War I, Mrs Humphry Ward, the novelist and Conservative, campaigned hard for London County Council financial support for her play centres. In fact the pattern of voluntary and statutory activity was unpredictable. Enid Fox (1993) has shown how the voluntary sector retained monopoly control of district nursing until as late as 1948, and Matthew Thomson (1992) has shown how voluntary organisations ceded control of mental institutions in 1913, but kept hold of care in the community. Thomson has described the relationships between the voluntary and statutory sectors in the field of mental health as 'symbiotic', with the Board of Control attempting to use the voluntary sector to overcome statutory limitations and the voluntary sector using this to gain a position of influence.

Relations between the state and voluntarism did become more blurred during the inter-war years. Hubert Llewellyn Smith, statistician and civil servant, spoke in 1937 of a 'borderland' rather than a borderline existing between them. Certainly there was a thoroughgoing attempt to reconceptualise the relationship between the sectors, which while it might have been in advance of the reality was influential and also signalled how far the COS had fallen behind the majority view in this respect. Constance Braithwaite, who owned that she was trying to reconcile her faith in philanthropy with her commitment to socialism, came out in favour of a 'national minimum': 'my conclusion is that the relief of poverty should be the responsibility of the State and not of charity, but that charitable relief will and should continue as long as poverty exists which is not adequately relieved by the state' (Braithwaite, 1938, p. 16). This left voluntary organisations, in her view, with a supplementary role, an experimental or pioneering role.

This position was not very different from Elizabeth Macadam's (1934) influential analysis of the 'new philanthropy', in which she called for closer cooperation between the state and voluntary organisations. The COS had called for the same from its foundation, but Macadam's notion of cooperation was significantly different. She welcomed the Webbs' idea of the 'extension ladder' as a prescription for voluntary/ statutory relations, which they expressed following the 1909 Royal Commission Report on the Poor Laws as part of their political campaign to break up the poor law. In other words, voluntary organisations would influence and supplement public services, but no longer aim to be the first line of defence for social service. Indeed, Macadam had special criticism for the COS, calling on it to 'frankly recognise' that the future could not lie in trying to supersede the state (Macadam, 1934, p. 67). Some of the new twentieth-century forms of voluntary personal social service societies – the guilds of help, which spread rapidly in the Edwardian years, and the councils of social service, which were more a feature of the inter-war period – were much more ready to cooperate with the state in the manner suggested by Macadam than was the COS. The actual work of these newer societies with their stress on personal social work had much in common with the COS, but Attlee (1920, p. 79) was probably correct when he highlighted the importance of their different 'outlook of spirit' and their more democratic tone. The idiom of the inter-war COS seemed to belong to an earlier age.

While a writer such as Henry Mess (1947), the director of Tyneside Council of Social Service during the depression years and then a reader in sociology at the University of London, could still envisage the possibility of the state and the voluntary sector agreeing on a division of labour – that is on a more complementary relationship – T.S. Simey (1937), a lecturer in public administration at Liverpool University, followed Macadam's lead in seeing nothing beyond a supplementary role for the voluntary sector. These were only prescriptions for voluntary organisations. They were not accurate descriptions of the pattern of voluntary action. However, by the end of the inter-war years, it is striking both how the balance between the state and voluntarism had shifted and how there was a vacuum when it came to justifying voluntary activity, the main idea being that voluntary organisations were useful for doing what the state could not manage to do.

To some extent this view was modified by commentators in the period following the Beveridge Report of 1942, although many local and national politicians remained relatively hostile or indifferent to the voluntary sector. Beveridge himself was a firm believer in voluntary action and harked back strongly to the turn of the century insistence on the importance of the 'spirit of service'; the good society could only be built on people's sense of duty and willingness to serve (Beveridge, 1948, pp. 151, 222, 320). Beveridge saw voluntary action as an important counterweight to the business motive and, like many others, as a fundamental ingredient of modern democracy. Voluntary organisations provided the opportunity for free association and participation, as well as variety and spontaneity (Lindsay, 1945). Later still, in the early 1970s, Richard Crossman (1976) came to the view that voluntary action was to be valued for its idealism and had a role to play in humanising state bureaucracies. However, voluntary organisations were still perceived as supplementary, or at best complementary, to the state and the desirability of direct provision by the state was not questioned. During the period of the classic welfare state, the relationship between economic growth and state social provision was believed to be positive. This resulted in a wholehearted commitment to state intervention to secure full employment, a redistributive social security system (although the actual extent of redistribution is debatable) that would enhance social consumption, and social services that were regarded as social investments.

The COS seemingly fell into line with the prevailing wisdom when the Beveridge Report was published: 'The Society is of the opinion that in the post-war world the community must accept responsibility for supplying the basic needs of its citizens' in respect of both income maintenance and social services (Beveridge, 1948, p. 148; Beveridge was invited to speak at the COS's 1943 annual general meeting). The COS had already taken on responsibility for running some of the Citizens' Advice Bureaux in London, which Beveridge was able to welcome as emblematic of the new voluntary effort, informing people about state services in the modern post-war democracy. However, the main body of COS work remained personal social work with individuals and families. This was reaffirmed when the Society changed its name in 1946 to the Family Welfare Association (FWA).

From the beginning, the COS had believed that the only sure way to achieve social change was to work to change the habits, attitudes and behaviour of individuals, although in practice much of its social work was undertaken in order to ascertain whether a family was worthy of material help outside the ambit of the poor law. The COS rejected what the Americans called 'wholesale' legislative change on behalf of masses as fundamentally unsound, and, whereas charity organisation societies in the late nineteenth and early twentieth-century United States found it possible to reconcile 'wholesale' and 'retail' (individual) methods of reform, the British COS never did so. The COS mounted a strong defence of personal social service as opposed to impersonal state welfare during the inter-war years, turning increasingly to the new psychology to do so. In one of his wilder flights of fancy, J.C. Pringle, the General Secretary of the COS for most of the inter-war period, declared social casework to be the answer to Bolshevism. Nor did the COS depart from its goal of providing a casework service to individuals in the post-war years, notwithstanding its new-found commitment to collective provision. The FWA built its reputation on its psychodynamic casework, the practice of which became increasingly specialised and wholly reliant on paid professional workers. The COS had been a pioneer in the training of social workers, denying that voluntarism had to mean amateurism. But the post-war FWA social workers tended to identify first and foremost with the elite corps of psychodynamically trained members of a profession, which was something new.

In 1948, Parliament agreed to abolish the poor law. Despite the COS/FWA's emphasis on social casework, it was so closely associated with the poor law that it was forced to rethink its purpose. The FWA had to relate to a new set of state social services which adhered to different principles and in which the number of social workers rapidly increased. It faced internal and external problems in its efforts to adjust to the new situation. First, the FWA had two distinct sides to it: social work with individuals and families, and the administration of relief funds. In the context of COS social theory, these had joined together to serve the same purpose. The relief funds were used if it was determined that an individual and his family could be helped back to self-maintenance by the injection of cash or material help in kind, but in the post-war world, where eligibility for national assistance was no longer determined by the deterrent principles of the poor law, the FWA was no longer helping a client group separate from that seeking state aid. The role of its relief funds had therefore to be rethought and, increasingly, as the social work profession sought to distance itself from involvement with money, the two arms of the FWA appeared more and more as separate empires.

Second, while the COS had had a firm idea of its relationship to the poor law, the FWA had to decide how to relate to the fragmented social services of the post-war years. The idea that the organisation might become a supplement to state services was not overly helpful. The FWA had traditionally provided a family service, but as Richard Titmuss (1954, p. 7) remarked, after the abolition of the poor law, post-war social services were moulded by the pattern of administrative structures and social work specialisation took place 'by skill, by function, by setting, by Whitley and by chance'. It was more possible for the FWA to present itself as complementary to state-provided social services, and increasingly it depended on its powers to persuade local government that its activities were worth funding.

Third, the post-war years saw major changes in state social services and in social work to which the FWA, struggling to come to terms with both its inherited historical traditions and the new demands of the post-war welfare state, found it difficult to respond. After the 1968 Seebohm Report on the personal social services and the establishment of social services departments which aimed to provide universal access, the FWA faced the issue of how to justify a specialised, social work service delivered to a small number of clients. In addition, while social work appeared to flourish in terms of increasing numbers and a clearer professional identity within the new social services departments, doubts about its effectiveness, and particularly of the kind of psychodynamically oriented social work that the FWA made its special province, continued to be expressed.[3] As many commentators have observed, the period of optimism that accompanied the Seebohm reforms was remarkably short-lived.

In many respects, the prospects for voluntary organisations generally appeared brighter after the election of the first Thatcher government in 1979. A more mixed economy of welfare received massive encouragement during the 1980s and 1990s, but in the context of a voluntary sector that relies heavily on paid as well as unpaid workers and a strongly centralising state. Late twentieth-century voluntary effort is no longer autonomous from that of the public sector. The lines have been blurred in terms of the use of paid staff and the receipt of state funding for much of the twentieth century. It is not therefore possible to think of voluntary provision re-emerging as the provider of first resort in the same manner as in the late nineteenth century.

The 'tight/loose' organisation pioneered by private sector firms in the 1980s, involving the decentralisation of production and the centralisation of command, has been paralleled in the 'new public management' of the public sector. Since 1988, 'quasi-markets' have been introduced in all the social services – in health, housing, education and community care – with the voluntary sector becoming a major provider in housing and community care and the private sector a bigger provider in education, while health remains more of an internal market. But central government has set the parameters; the fiscal conditions have been set by the centre. This makes the mixed economy of the late twentieth century very different from the mixed economy of the late nineteenth. Because post-war service-providing voluntary agencies have been funded primarily by government, their room for manoeuvre in the new situation is limited. While government has held out a larger role for them in social provision, government is also in a position to say what it will contract with them to do. The FWA has not been alone in having to tailor what it offers to what local government is prepared to buy, which differs from place to place. Voluntary organisations may be in the process of becoming alternative (rather than supplementary or complementary) providers of welfare. But a situation in which the state determines the conditions of provision without taking responsibility is new. This form of welfare pluralism does not position voluntary agencies as mediating institutions, but tends rather to see them as instruments of the state, which raises difficult questions for agencies about both identity and function.

Geoffrey Finlayson (1990) has used the concept of 'a moving frontier' to describe the relationship between the voluntary and the statutory sector. It may be more useful to take the rather flabby term 'partnership' as a way of conceptualising this relationship. The idea of partnership was invoked by the 1952 Nathan Committee on charitable trusts and traced back to the beginning of the twentieth century (Cmd 8710). The Nathan Committee used the term to describe what it viewed as a cooperative and essentially cosy relationship between the two sectors. In fact from its earliest days the COS may be said to have worked in partnership with the state, but the way in which it envisaged cooperation had nothing to do with playing a supplementary or complementary role. Nor have the 1990s ideas of a 'contract culture' partnership much in common with the kind of relationship voluntary organisations providing services had with their local authorities under grant aid in the post-war period.

It is possible to look at the development of the COS and FWA only in terms of the kind of work they performed (Woodroofe, 1962). Certainly the changing nature of social work within the organisation carries a significance that stretches beyond the organisation itself. However, an analysis of the organisation's positioning within the wider world of social provision is crucial to an understanding of its fortunes.

## NOTES

1. Esping Andersen's idea of a Scandinavian model also breaks down when gender is introduced as a variable (Leira, 1992).
2. I have tended to use 'voluntary sector' as a collective noun. 'Charity' was given a particular meaning by the COS, which is explored further in Chapter 1. It should also be noted that, by the inter-war period, charity had become pejorative in a way that philanthropy and voluntarism never did, in part because of its association with the claims and practice of the COS.
3. Even at the end of the 1950s, when official reports were agreed on the need to train and employ more social workers, doubts as to their efficacy were expressed (Wootton, 1959). Savage indictments have continued to arise periodically, for example Brewer and Lait (1980).

# PART I
# The COS

# 1. Early ideals, 1870–1918

## THE IDEA OF CHARITY

Charity meant something special to the COS. It was conceived of as a fundamental social principle crucial to the health and progress of society. The leaders of the COS wrote extensively about their new conception of charity, but part of the problem of the Society was that its ideas were never fully understood either by the world outside or, indeed, by many of its own members. The understanding of most of the women visitors, whose personal work with poor families was so important as the vehicle for implementing the new ideas about charity as a means of achieving social progress, got no further than a generalised sympathy with the poor or a sense of what was owed to the poor by the better off. Even among the leading members of the COS there was something of a divide between people like Charles Stuart Loch, the influential secretary of the Society from 1875 to 1914, and Bernard Bosanquet, academic philosopher and member of the Council of the London COS, whose work was central in reformulating charity as a social principle, and those such as Thomas Mackay and W.A. Bailward, who were more inclined to frame the COS within the much narrower and harsher principles of classical political economy.[1]

Loch and Bosanquet insisted that charity was not philanthropy. Loch repeated time and again that the COS was not just another relief society; charity was not merely a matter of the rich giving money to the poor. More relief, more money, more begging letters did not amount to charitable work and Loch felt alienated from those members of the COS who talked only in terms of cooperating with the poor law and of charity as a means of curbing pauperism.[2] He spoke instead of charity as having social purpose and being the 'central mood of the good life' (Loch, 1923, p. 89). Loch spelled out what he meant by this most clearly in a paper he wrote in 1910 on the ethics of charity. The goal of charity was the promotion of a sense of membership in society. The practice of charity was centred on the nature of the obligations attaching to that membership and the ways in which a particular individual could be enabled to participate as a citizen. The basic conditions of membership, or citizenship, were that an individual must become socially efficient, that is self-sustaining and morally competent. For Bernard Bosanquet (1899), the behaviour of people within their families – whether they were capable of caring for and supporting each other – was the test of citizenship and an ethical state. Furthermore, the fulfilment of citizenship obligations in an ethical state had to be voluntary, which was why charity and not the statutory authorities was accorded such importance. People had to act morally of their own free will; by definition they could not be forced to do so. Charity thus had less to do with poverty *per se* than with social efficiency and participation (Loch, 1923) and charity became ethical because it had this social purpose.

E.J. Urwick (1912), who began work as a district secretary for the COS in 1893 and took over direction of its School of Sociology in 1903, also stressed the importance of charity as social purpose. It was purposive striving that made any social policy worthwhile because it ensured that it was consciously directed towards the spiritual good. This test of policy against purpose could have been endorsed by social reformers across a wide political spectrum; R.H. Tawney, for example, would have shared it. But people like Loch, Bosanquet and Urwick were distinguished by their conviction that *charity* was a fundamental social principle, whose practice offered the possibility of achieving real and sustainable social progress.

It would probably be mistaken to claim that this view of charity prevailed in the Society. At crucial moments, such as the debate over the 1909 Report of the Royal Commission on the Poor Laws, it became clear that the 'harder and dryer' views within the Society had the edge. It is nevertheless important to understand what the idealists in the Society wanted because it is their conviction as to the possibilities of charity that explains both the power of the Society's public voice and why it held to its ideas, especially in terms of the role of the state, when the external environment began to change significantly.

The old idea of charity was that it consisted of spontaneous and free giving from rich to poor. But if charity was to succeed in its new-found social purpose it had to be disciplined. Loch explained that 'at first sight the words charity and organisation seem to be a contradiction in terms. Charity is free, independent, fervent, compulsive. Organisation implies order and method, sacrifice for a common end, self-restraint' (Loch, 1893, p. 153). The COS attempted to draw these together – to appeal to intelligence as well as devotion, to knowledge as well as to love. Thus it had to find new working principles and new ways in which to work. At the theoretical level, the COS had to seek to reconcile the older religious motivation to love one's neighbour and the poor with the doctrines of the classical economists, who warned of the perils of public and voluntary expenditure on the poor, which would in their view only serve further to demoralise and pauperise. Following the ideas of the Reverend T.R. Malthus and his famous 'law of population', economists believed that population tended to outrun subsistence, a state of affairs that could only be exacerbated by giving the poor money which would allow them to subsist and further procreate. Lacking a theory of demand, classical economic theory could only envisage expenditure on the poor as essentially unproductive. Poverty in and of itself was regarded as inevitable and something of a spur to effort. The evil was pauperism, or destitution, the causes of which were believed to lie with the individual rather than in situations and structures beyond the individual's control. Thus pauperism became in large measure a moral issue even within economic theory.

All leaders of the COS subscribed in large measure to these views, especially regarding the causes of pauperism. All were convinced as to the evils of indiscriminate charity, which offered alms to whomever applied and threatened to undermine the deterrent poor law, and of the need to organise charity such that it worked harmoniously alongside the poor law in the manner dictated by the Goschen Minute.[3] However, for Loch and Bosanquet true charity meant more than the application of the principles of political economy. They strove to reconcile older Christian views about charity with the science of economics in order to reach a new synthesis. Indeed, Loch and Bosanquet were at pains to distinguish their idea of charity from simple political economy. As Bosanquet put it:

> A moral point of view does not mean a point of view which holds a question as solved by apportioning blame to the unfortunate; it does mean a point of view which treats men not as economic abstractions, but as living selves with a history and ideas and a character of their own. (Bosanquet, 1895b, p.105)

Bosanquet (1901) firmly rejected the idea that a training for personal social service among the poor could be grounded solely in economics. Ethics were far more important than economic theory in distinguishing the purpose of charity; Urwick (1912) believed that nine-tenths of the mistakes of economists were due to their effort to consider economic man in isolation from moral man. Loch regretted the way in which John Ruskin had placed social affection on one side and political economy on the other, and argued instead that love could not be love 'if it did not seek to found itself on knowledge' (Loch, 1923, p.102). For charity to have a social purpose it required a social discipline: 'it works through sympathy; it depends on science; and in fervency it is religious' (Loch, 1904, p. 189).

All members of the COS could agree that their practice of charity needed to become 'scientific', meaning that they had to examine their practices carefully so that the Society did not become just one more relief society. But to some, like Mackay and Bailward, the pull of the doctrines of economic science, which stressed the negative and deterrent aspects of relief, played a more important part than Loch and Bosanquet's desire to reconcile religious and economic ideas, such that love was informed by knowledge. Bailward (1908), the honorary secretary of the Bethnal Green COS between 1887 and 1918 and also member and sometime chair of the local board of guardians, stoutly defended giving charity the leading role in matters to do with relief because – and here he echoed John Stuart Mill – it was a superior instrument to the state in that the poor could never claim relief as a right. In this account, charity was important chiefly for the way in which it might serve to limit the operations of the poor law. Thomas Mackay (1896), a council member of the London COS who wrote extensively on the poor law, believed that the law operated on collectivist principles and that charity alone coalesced with market principles of automatic and natural adjustment.

Loch himself was a strongly committed Christian. The diary he kept during his early years with the COS reveals a constant battle for religious understanding. He experienced a piercing conviction of sin and a strong sense of the importance of compassion, of 'suffering with those to whom the loving act is done'.[4] But, like so many late Victorians, he was worried about the compatibility of religion with science. Given that science could prove that the miracles and resurrection did not take place, in what sense was the Bible true?[5] Loch's predicament was not unusual among late Victorian thinkers. Mrs Humphry Ward, the extremely successful novelist, also found herself unable to accept religious dogma, not because of science so much as the rise of historical criticism, which seemed to show that there was no single way of seeing and no one truth. T.H. Green, the Oxford idealist philosopher who had a great impact on both Ward and Loch, who was one of his pupils, taught that criticism and religion could be reconciled. Green reached the point where religion consisted of giving expression to the life of Jesus in our everyday lives. The individual was not asked to imitate Christ but, rather, God became immanent in everyday duties and personal lives (Vincent, 1986). It thus became crucial to link theory and action, which Loch and Bosanquet did through their particular conceptualisation of charity. Again like Ward, Loch was rather disillusioned with organised religion and its propensity to use charitable relief in the competition for converts.[6] For Loch, the proper expression of a religiously inspired love and compassion for the poor consisted of a careful inquiry into their circumstances and the formulation of a plan of action that would enable them to become self-maintaining and fully participative citizens.

Scientific knowledge, particularly in the form of economics, made Loch and other members of the COS interrogate the nature of the gift. In his diary, Loch worried briefly as to whether science in the form of social Darwinism dictated that the weak should be sacrificed.[7] This was the view of a militant individualist such as Herbert Spencer. In her diary, the young Beatrice Webb, who was much influenced by Spencer, recorded the view that, no matter how it was practised, charitable relief must favour the weak to the detriment of the strong.[8] This made it all the more important that charitable work be planned and well-organised so that it did not merely permit the socially inefficient to subsist.

Loch was more concerned as to whether charity might not in fact be selfish. Certainly the old charity could be so described. Loch felt that all too often the rich did not really care for the poor. It was all too easy to give some money, but this amounted to little more than the salving of the consciences of the rich and to this extent was selfish.[9] Giving to the poor at Christmas, for example, did not constitute real charity; it was, in Loch's view, prompted by the contrast between rich and poor, not by love and the idea of giving up one's own life for one's friend.[10] But then Loch was also worried that self-sacrifice might represent selfishness rather than altruism. Again, the answer to this seemed to lie in purposive striving. It was important not to look for results, but just to seek to 'do right'. By striving for the good life, the means became the end.[11] As Octavia Hill, the pioneering housing reformer and founding member of the COS, wrote to her friend and co-worker Henrietta Barnett in 1873: 'I fight so desperately to be right, to see right, to do right'.[12] Mackay also distrusted altruism but on the grounds that it caused 'promiscuous benevolence', and urged that the proper business of altruism (and hence charity) was to help the poor get property (Mackay, 1889, p. 285).

For Hill and Loch right action relied on 'right feeling'. This came from the sincere pursuit of the social good. To those of her followers who worried as to whether they had interpreted God's will correctly, Hill offered some comfort: 'the burden of absolutely right action ... is not with you, only the duty of trying to see and do right'.[13] Stefan Collini (1991) has shown the importance of altruism and feeling in late Victorian social thought. Because it was widely believed that men's inclinations were selfish, doing one's duty became very important. Duty was pitted against inclination and will against appetite. The search was for an ethics that, while not divorced from religion, was not dependent on religious dogma. As Gertrude Himmelfarb (1986, p. 74) has remarked, the English made a religion of morality and they 'made a social ethic of individual morality'. George Eliot said that, while God was inconceivable, duty was absolute (ibid., p. 21). Feelings were perceived to be the source of right action and T.H. Green's teaching was a systematic expression of the sensibility that finds something repugnant in self-regarding actions (Collini, 1991).

The attempt by COS leaders to reconcile science and religion became a sum greater than the parts. Social theory and social action assumed a strongly spiritual dimension. Nowhere was this more clear than in the writing of Urwick, who opposed any unicausal explanation of social phenomena and who, while wishing to introduce students to social science, wanted also to stress that social science had 'to be subordinate to a philosophy of life which passes boldly beyond the dominion of any science' (Urwick, 1912, p. vi). This view was echoed by Bernard Bosanquet (1898), when he wrote of the importance of the faith that the world of facts has an idea, a principle, an order and organisation. The true explanation and justification of social change had to be sought in philosophy, not science.

For Loch and Bosanquet, the key to the practice of true charity lay in the principle of reciprocity. According to Loch: 'as price is the measure of economic exchange, so at the time or ultimately a rise in the standard of membership [of society] is the measure of the social exchange, which we call reciprocity' (Loch, 1923, p. 47). While justice emphasised *individual* rights and duties of membership of a society, Loch's view of charity stressed the social interdependence of people, their need for service, friendly dealing and 'social solidarity' (Loch, 1923,

p. 69; 1910, p. 372). Bernard Bosanquet's idea of democratic citizenship was based on the idea of the innumerable obligations of citizens one to the other. Citizens were independent and in a society founded on the principles of true charity gave service to one another voluntarily (Bosanquet, 1910). In Bosanquet's view, the better off were performing their obligations as citizens when they (voluntarily) offered the poor help, not just in the form of alms, but of personal service designed to promote self-maintenance and fully participative citizenship. The poor fulfilled their duties as citizens by responding to whatever plan was proposed to restore them to self-maintenance. The principle of reciprocity guarded against purely selfish actions on the part of the rich. It lifted charity above the narrow concerns of political economy and gave it ethical purpose. It implied face-to-face interaction between giver and recipient that would, it was hoped, bring the social classes together and create a socially efficient society, and it made the practice of personal social work integral to social theory. Whether it was possible to implement the principle of reciprocity was another matter. As Stedman Jones (1976) has pointed out, it was hard to see the relationship between poor families and COS workers as one of genuine social exchange. The traditional categories of donor and recipient more accurately described the relationship and also made it difficult to promote the kind of independent, self-sustaining behaviour on the part of the poor that the COS wanted to see.

In Loch and Bosanquet's formulation of charity, merely giving money did not constitute healthy social exchange; it might in fact represent selfish behaviour and it certainly ran counter to the prescriptions of classical economics. Octavia Hill wrote early on about what constituted helpful and unhelpful gifts. She stressed that it was important to give thought, time and heart, as well as money. The worker had to be prepared to give thought to the circumstances of the poor and to take the time both to consider how to help them and to see the plan of action through. The plan for help might or might not include the gift of money; either way the help had to be offered in a loving and sympathetic manner (Hill, 1877a). In 1889 she wrote a paper on the role of the COS, condemning the old charity which lacked principle and method, and asking whether alms were all that it was possible to give: 'where is the honest manly sympathy? where the exchange of ideas? where the natural neighbourliness which makes the friendships in our own class? and why are the friendships with our poorer neighbours to be so different?' (Hill, 1889, p. 17). Both Hill and Helen Bosanquet, who, before her marriage to Bernard Bosanquet in 1895, served as a district secretary for the COS (she went on to write extensively on social work and to edit the *Charity Organisation Review* between 1909 and 1921), stressed that all duties had to be performed thoroughly and that charity carried special responsibilities because it directly affected the lives of other human beings (Hill, 1898; Dendy, 1893).

The new ideas about charity proved extremely influential. In 1891, the Archbishop of Canterbury (1891, p.1) wrote a paper on the science of charity in which he declared, 'It is an evil thing to be charitable for the sake of giving careless and idle relief to one's feelings.' This showed that he had accepted the idea that the old philanthropic charity was essentially selfish and that a more scientific approach was needed. As Humphreys (1991) has noted, the lower echelons of the clergy were much less likely to adopt COS views about the poor and how to help them; however, the power of the COS derived from its ability to influence opinion makers. In fact, the Archbishop's understanding of the new charity was partial in that he emphasised the wrongs of indiscriminate giving without talking either about the importance of charity's social purpose – its larger goal – or the importance of giving in ways that did not necessarily include money. This kind of summary of the COS's ideas was prevalent and had more in common with those who stressed the importance of learning the lessons of classical political economy than with the views of Loch and Bosanquet. It also made it all too easy for people to agree as to the evils of giving alms without necessarily ensuring that they gave help to the poor in the form of love, sympathy and time. It was, in short, in some measure responsible for the 'hard and dry' image that the COS rapidly achieved.

Loch, Bosanquet, Urwick and Hill all accepted the tenets of political economy but deplored the notion that charity could be based on economic theory alone. In his diary for 1877, Loch feared that the 'non compromise party' had too much power: 'We must get more "heart" in it [the COS]'.[14] In his view charity needed 'the heart of a Dickens and the head and will of a Bismarck'.[15] All strands of COS opinion could agree that charity meant something different from mere almsgiving (for example, Bailward, 1920), but there can be no doubt that the idealist school of Loch and Bosanquet failed to get their message regarding the nature of charity across to a wider public. It was complicated, involving above all ideas about the nature of citizenship and its reciprocal duties and the importance of enabling the poor to become fully participative members of society. In the end it was hopelessly idealistic, not least because it relied on the voluntary principle. The problem was that, without a firm commitment to charity as a social principle grounded in ideas of interdependence and reciprocity, COS ideas tended to be reduced to stopping the flow of indiscriminate charity, which in turn was likely to make COS practice harsh.

## THE IDEA OF SOCIAL WORK

The practice of the new charity relied on personal social service, what was usually called 'friendly visiting' in the late nineteenth century. The term 'social work' began to be used in the 1890s and tended to be used interchangeably with 'casework', indicating that personal social service had come to mean, in theory at least, the careful and sympathetic investigation of the applicant's case and the formulation of a plan of treatment. The practice of personal social work was believed to be the means of achieving the kind of social progress envisaged by the new charity. Lasting reform could only be achieved by changing people. Social workers would work with individuals and their families to change their habits, build up their characters and give new purpose to their lives. Individual social work was above all a form of education and had the additional advantage that it sprang from the self-development of middle-class people to the point where they responded voluntarily to the noble impulse of fulfilling their obligations to their fellow citizens.

The central place given to social work shows the distance between members of the COS and unrelenting *laissez-faire* individualists, such as Herbert Spencer. The COS did not believe in standing back from the problem of poverty, and Bernard Bosanquet (1890) rejected the idea of an opposition between individualism and collectivism, preferring to see them as positions on a spectrum of ideas. While the COS was committed to voluntary rather than statutory social work, there existed, as Collini has observed, a hegemonic set of assumptions regarding duty and service to others (Collini, 1979, p. 49). The commitment to voluntary social work was a commitment to social action. In fact, to the COS and to many other social reformers of the late nineteenth and early twentieth centuries, individualism meant something more than anti-statism, referring to the preference for tackling social problems by treating the needs of individuals in a holistic fashion within the context of the family, as well as for keeping state intervention to a minimum. In Loch's view, 'the key to success in charity lies in persistent care for the individual in close connection with the family and in discerning and friendly aid, according to the needs of the particular case' (Loch, 1904, p. 5). The test of charity was the successful promotion of economic independence and fully participative citizens (Loch, 1923). Social work with individuals and families was the means of achieving this; no social advance was possible without individual improvement.

The idea of 'friendly visiting' was significantly different from the older nineteenth-century concept of district visiting, which was usually based on the parish and involved visitors taking responsibility for a geographical area. Friendly visitors were assigned families (Loch, 1892) and were told to 'befriend, aid and elevate' the people they visited (COS, 1870). Octavia Hill and, later, Helen Bosanquet did the most to develop the idea of friendly visiting in the early decades of the COS. This reflected the gendered division of labour within the COS, whereby men predominated on the committees and women did the visiting. Hill, but not Helen Bosanquet, was additionally impatient with the kind of theorising about charity that Loch and Bernard Bosanquet engaged in, laying much more store by the lessons of 'quiet, practical work' with the poor (Hill, 1877a, p. 5).

Hill was convinced that the older form of district visitors were all too ready to offer relief. They approached their task with religious tracts in one hand and tickets entitling the household to some form of relief in the other. On the other hand, tracts without a coal ticket when the grate was empty seemed to indicate a want of sympathy. No principle informed their relief practices and no uniform system of administration governed their work. Hill graphically described the position of the average district visitor:

> I wonder whether you have among you instances of the solitary, inexperienced district visitor, and can feel for her difficulties? Do you know what I mean? A lady, well born, highly cultivated, well nurtured, becomes convinced that she has duties to the poor. Perhaps some great personal pain drives her to seek refuge from it in Christian service of the poor; perhaps some family loss darkens her whole horizon, and opens her eyes to other forms of sorrow; perhaps some stirring sermon startles her in the midst of triumphant pleasure, making her feel that she ought to give some slight offering of time to the poor; perhaps wariness of all superficial glitter of amusement makes her seek for deeper interests in life ... She does not start with the desire of knowing the poor but of helping them ... She does not think of them primarily as people, but as poor people. (Hill, 1877b, p. 48)

The first lesson for friendly visitors was to befriend the poor, rather than to approach them as people in need of assistance. This immediately called the practice of mixing relief with visiting into question, because, as Hill put it, 'doles darkened friendship' (Hill, 1877a, p. 60). What was really needed was people prepared to spend time with the poor, getting to know their real needs and how best they might be helped. Hill bade potential COS visitors to 'decide for yourselves quietly what amount of time you are justified in devoting to such work' (Hill, 1898, p. 237). Charity was a duty and all duties had to be done thoroughly, but the first call on women's time had to be their own families, hence the importance of thinking through their commitment.

Hill instructed friendly visitors that they should first give 'sympathetic, imaginative consideration' to the case to see what the causes of the problem were: 'he is worth no one's money; he is ill and needs cure; or he is idle or ignorant, or bad tempered, and needs – my friends, what does he need?' (Hill, 1889, p. 17). She warned that it was never easy to help a member of one's own family and that the difficulties would be greater still when dealing with strangers, but that it would help the visitor if she tried to deal with the poor as she would a family member. Too much help and the person needing assistance would become dependent, too little and he would lose hope. Irregular visiting and alms only served to keep 'a whole class' on the brink of pauperism when they might be taught the self-control and foresight that would allow them to improve their position. Friendly visitors were told to help adult men in the household to find work, to help them to save, to lend them books and to teach them to appreciate art and nature. However, her injunction not to give cash to the able-bodied poor was susceptible to extremely narrow interpretation. Hill recognised this when she warned that the philosophy of the new charity did not mean that the rich could cultivate their own elegant tastes 'in happy satisfaction that the poor cannot be bettered by our gifts [and] in fact must learn self-help' (Hill, 1877b, p. 90). But, as early as 1869, Ruskin warned that she laid too much emphasis on the evil of almsgiving and not enough on the importance of the gift of time and personal sympathy. He felt that, had she put the latter point more strongly to her audience, comprised in 1869 of the Association for the Promotion of Social Science, she would not have found them so enthusiastic.[16]

Hill was aware that without the visitors as the 'living links' in the system COS practices appeared 'dry and formal' (Hill, 1872, p. 444). Visiting was personal and intimate and she stressed what it meant to poor families to be known rather than numbered (Hill, 1875, p. 58). Individual work, she believed, would serve to re-establish 'natural human intercourse' between rich and poor and would also serve to reveal the facts of life among the poor to what she feared was a largely sentimental public.[17]

It is easy to be scornful of Hill's injunction to visitors to befriend the poor. At the end of the day the aim of the visitor was to bring about change in the households she visited. As Hill put it: 'my only notion of reform is that of living side by side with people, till all that one believes becomes clear to them' (Maurice, 1928, p. 211). The social work she engaged in was 'detailed' and consisted of 'infinitesimally small actions' (Hill, 1869, p. 222) designed to change the way in which the poor behaved. Hill insisted that good social work was not paternalistic: all people, rich and poor, had to come to their own decisions as to what constituted right action, it could not be imposed from above. The visitor could not learn the true cause of a family's difficulty until she was prepared to care for that family, no easy task in the noisy, smelly courts of late nineteenth-century London. With friendship came trust and then the visitor could be sure that the people were ready to listen. In her work of housing management, Hill believed that trust grew not just out of friendship but out of the fulfilment of the mutual obligations of landlord and tenant, out of the business relationship. In friendly visiting, the visitor was supposed to gain the household's trust and then lead by example. But in the end the visitor was expected to try and get poor families to see the virtues of middle-class values and culture. In Geoffrey Best's (1964) judgement, the poor were helped if they would submit.

Nevertheless, the friendly visitor was encouraged to respect the people she visited and to treat them with courtesy. Hill told her rent collectors that they must 'show the same respect for the privacy and independence and should treat them with the same courtesy that I should show towards other personal friends' (Hill, 1875, p. 77). How far social workers followed this instruction, even to the extent of knocking on a door before entering, is not clear, for the same sort of advice was constantly repeated by social work leaders throughout the late nineteenth and early twentieth centuries (for example, Kanthack, 1907).

But the women who played such a large role in conceptualising early social work did have a considerable sympathy with and understanding of the lifestyles of poor families and particularly of the women in those families. In her writing Helen Bosanquet strove to help social workers understand the world view of the poor. Like many late nineteenth-century social investigators, she was convinced as to the central importance of the working class wife to the comfort of the family as a whole. In her first book she spoke of their 'patient endurance, unceasing sacrifice and terrible devotion' (Bosanquet, 1896, p. 107). She recognised the difficulty of budgeting on an irregular income and of avoiding the temptation of credit. She demonstrated a thorough knowledge of the options of borrowing, pawning and delaying payment and her estimate of the rates of interest involved – 24 per cent for pawnbrokers and up to 400 per cent for private money-lenders – has been confirmed by a recent historical study (Tebbut, 1983). She knew how it was that a costermonger's business practices forced him to use credit and how a housewife might use the pawnbroker as a way of equalising income. And she appreciated the problems of cooking on an open fire and condemned the typical ignorance of the well-meaning philanthropist of the limitations that this imposed on the choice of menus. She also drew attention to the difficulty of communication between middle-class social workers and the poor, and the difficulty social workers would experience in knowing how their advice was being received and interpreted.

But the purpose of visiting, befriending and investigating the circumstances of the household and the reasons for the difficulties that were being experienced was to work with the family in order to change their habits and behaviour. In an essay on the meaning of social work, Bernard Bosanquet wrote that social workers usually wanted to brighten lives and improve conditions. But it was important for all prospective social workers to realise that improving conditions effectively meant changing matters so that the poor were able to make more of their lives than they did before, in other words so that their characters would be able to master their circumstances: 'wherever you start in social work the goal is the same – to bring the social mind into order, into harmony with itself ... social disorganisation is the outward and visible form of moral and intellectual disorganisation' (Bosanquet, 1901, p. 297). Loch[18] and the Bosanquets acknowledged that both rich and poor could lack character. Bernard Bosanquet wrote that the 'spirit of pauperism' could be found in all social classes, manifesting itself in a weakness of mind (Bosanquet, 1910, p. 398). And Helen added that the lives of the rich as much as those of the poor could be 'one incoherent jumble from beginning to end' (Dendy, 1895b, p. 83). However, wealth allowed the pauper spirit to exist without evidence of pauperisation; in the poor, pauperisation became immediately visible. The Bosanquets insisted on the democratic nature of their conception of character, but, because the poor were in danger of becoming a public charge, attention focused exclusively on them. The apparent inability of the poor to think ahead, to save for periods of sickness or unemployment, for example, was regularly cited as evidence of moral and intellectual disorganisation and failing of character. The process of strengthening the sense of obligations between people and particularly between family members, which was at the centre of the conceptualisation of the new charity, translated into social work practice as the work of building character among poor families.

As Collini has pointed out, the idea of character depended on a prior notion of duty, and invocations of character 'in fact presupposed an agreed moral code' (Collini, 1985, pp. 36–7). Unlike Helen and Bernard Bosanquet, Octavia Hill did not spend time elaborating the idea of character and its importance. She simply assumed, in common with the vast majority of legislators and policy makers of the late nineteenth and early twentieth centuries, that 'habits' were a crucial determinant of social status. She felt that the constant need to judge character was both the most crucial and the most difficult part of her work in housing. As she told the Royal Commission on working-class housing in the mid-1880s: 'The management depends very much on judgement of character. You must notice when the man is doing any better and when he is not' (C.4402-I, Q.8865). A large part of knowing the poor meant knowing their characters, but

> by knowledge of character more is meant than whether a man is a drunkard or a woman is dishonest, it means knowledge of the passions, hopes and history of people; where the temptation will touch them, what is the little scheme they have made of their lives, or would make, if they had encouragement, what training long-past phases of their lives may have afforded; how to move, touch, teach them. (Maurice, 1913, p. 258)

Bernard and Helen Bosanquet devoted considerable effort to exploring why and to a lesser extent how social workers should work to address the central issue of character. In an essay written for a collection edited by Jane Addams, the famous Chicago settlement house pioneer, Bernard Bosanquet stressed the importance of working with the individual to a plan based on 'respect for character' (B. Bosanquet, 1893, p. 250). He held that individual character was the most important determinant of the individual's circumstances, although he was at pains to stress that this did not mean attributing all blame for a person's position to that person and leaving him to his fate. That would have been the attitude of *laissez-faire* individualists, but idealists were eager to provide the means to help those in need by strengthening their characters, which according to their analysis was where the real problem lay, rather than in poverty *per se*. Bernard Bosanquet anticipated the need for large numbers of volunteer social workers to help their fellow citizens who found themselves in distress: 'you offer everything – the whole matériel and guidance of life ... there is as it were, an army of social healers to be trained and organised ... disciplined and animated with a single spirit and purpose...' (B. Bosanquet, 1909, p.115).

Bosanquet felt that building character would effect a much more lasting improvement than changing economic circumstances, which could result in change for the better only if character was also improved. The favourite example used by the COS was that of the drunkard who would merely spend any alms on more drink unless he could be successfully rehabilitated first. But Helen Bosanquet also drew on rather more subtle examples. Comparing five families she observed across the back garden of her East London house in the early 1890s (when she was serving as a district secretary for the COS), she noted that the children of number 4 lived in the same surroundings and had the opportunity to go to the same school and yet were in a much more distressed condition than their neighbours. She concluded that it was 'wholesome home atmosphere' that was wanting, clearly a case where the inculcation of good habits rather than money was what was needed (Dendy, 1895a, p.32). It became the task of social work to repair will and build character.

The Bosanquets and the COS generally were often accused of ignoring circumstances altogether. Bernard Bosanquet saw character 'as a name for life as it looks, when you take it as all connected together; circumstance is a name for life as it looks when you take it bit by bit' (Bosanquet, 1901, p. 302). It was not so much that the leaders of the COS ignored the importance of circumstances, but that character was believed to be the more fundamental issue. Helen Bosanquet argued that a man's circumstances depended on what he himself was. It was therefore 'man himself' who had to be changed if his 'circumstances are to be avoided' (Bosanquet, 1903a, p. 55). The desire to spend money wisely and to seek 'higher pleasures' and a 'higher standard' of life had to come from within. This was why both the Bosanquets and Loch exhibited impatience with the methods of late nineteenth-century social investigators, such as Charles Booth and Benjamin Seebohm Rowntree, who sought to establish the incidence of poverty in London and York, respectively. Helen Bosanquet felt that the 'poverty lines' drawn by the social investigators had 'a false air of definiteness' about them (Bosanquet, 1903b, p. 1). She could not accept Rowntree's conclusion that there was evidence of structural poverty in York resulting from low wages alone and quite independent of character (McKibbin, 1978). Similarly, Loch (1910) argued that social habit was as much a social fact as income, but Booth and Rowntree lacked any analysis of social habit, that is not just of income but how it was used. Urwick was concerned that Helen Bosanquet in particular was too eager wholly to subordinate social conditions to character (Urwick, 1903), but he too believed that 'social conditions come to matter less as formative influences as the individual and the race develop; and that the supra-social powers of the individual come to matter more as the formative factors to which the changes of social conditions are due' (Urwick, 1912, p. 41).

Kirkman-Gray, a contemporary who looked favourably on the extension of state intervention, believed that the COS's scientific theory of charity became 'an attempt to formulate a doctrine of human nature' (Kirkman-Gray, 1908, p. 114). Certainly, the evidence that Helen Bosanquet gleaned from her study of psychology allowed her to put all her faith in character and virtually none in structural causes. However, character was not an entirely 'market-oriented' concept, focusing exclusively on the importance of thrift, foresight, economic independence and self-control, as some historians have suggested (Fido, 1977), and as the invocation of personal responsibility – a concept closely allied to that of character – has become during the last decade. The centrality of character in idealist thought stemmed from the belief that the self-maintaining, independent citizen, possessed in other words of good character, was also the rational citizen, aware of common social purposes and struggling to realise what T.H. Green called his 'best self'. The emphasis on character was thus related to the idea of charity as a social principle and the desire to create purposive and participative citizens.

In the crucial process of the formation of character and purpose, mental struggle was considered the most important factor. It was, declared Helen Bosanquet (1897, p. 271), 'the first law of progress'. Mind and will were the makings of character. Social workers had to understand how these might be changed and Helen Bosanquet turned to the new science of psychology for help. The first step to changing the individual's will and creating a purposeful and active citizen was to make an effort to understand the individual's perceptions of his or her condition. The social worker had to be able to work out why it was that people saw things the way they did, to appreciate the values they held and then work with them to change their views and behaviour. No misfortune, no matter how distressing, was irredeemable until the individual's will was broken.

The poor had to be persuaded to raise their 'standard of life'. According to Bernard Bosanquet (1895b), all except the hopelessly degraded had an idea of what constituted an acceptable social standard. The crucial point was that standards were progressive. Helen Bosanquet used G.H. Stout's psychology (Stout was a colleague of Bernard Bosanquet at St Andrews University) to argue that man could be distinguished from the lower animals by his progressive wants. In lower animals the possession of instinct served to stop progressive development. Lacking instincts, man was left free to break the 'elementary cycle of appetites', by the recognition and pursuit of interests, particularly within the family unit; these enabled human beings to organise their minds purposively (Bosanquet, 1903a, p. 9). However, some people failed to develop progressive wants, being satisfied to eat, drink and sleep. In such people, habit performed much the same function as instinct in animals. Helen Bosanquet argued that the question of habit was very much one of training and education. If a wrong habit was acquired, then interests were not pursued. The duty of the social worker was therefore to correct bad habits and to foster the development of the kind of interests that would enable the raising of individual standards. Helen Bosanquet deplored the Malthusian 'economics of despair' and the theory of classical economists that wages tended to subsistence, believing that working people had a large capacity for self-improvement and social and economic advancement. She also believed that progressive wants, which made individuals raise their standards, led to constant emulation of their social superiors, with the result that there was more of a basis for class cooperation than class struggle.

The family occupied a special place in the Bosanquets' arguments regarding human motivation and behaviour. To the Bosanquets, as to T.H. Green, social awareness was built up through the family which was seen above all as the primary institution in which character was developed and in which cooperative individuals and rational citizens were produced. The Bosanquets were as convinced as Octavia Hill of the importance of the family and shared her conviction both that social work had to take place with individuals in their family context, and that the most useful social worker was likely to be a woman who had had experience of caring for family members. In Helen Bosanquet's last major book, *The Family* (1906), she argued that the Family (always capitalised) was the fundamental social unit. Its importance lay in the part it played in stimulating the interests of the individual. 'Natural' affection between husband and wife, and between parent and child ensured that homes became 'nurseries of citizenship' (B. Bosanquet, 1895a, p. 10). In *The Family*, Helen Bosanquet argued that the natural interest of family members in each other's welfare was a more powerful tie binding families together than economic considerations, patriarchal power or primitive maternal instinct. Through the altruistic love that naturally characterised family relations, individuals achieved consciousness of their unity with others. The family stood as a 'half-way house', mediating between the individual and the community. A strong citizenry and a strong state depended on the strengthening of the bonds between the individual and the family and between the family and the wider community. Given the enormity of its role in developing character, the importance of protecting and strengthening the family became one of the most dominant themes in the literature of the COS. Thus the work of the voluntary sector in the provision was fused with that of the family.

In a manner remarkably like the structural functionalist theory of the 1950s, the family was seen as playing the crucial role in socialising the individual (Parsons and Bales, 1955). Helen Bosanquet drew heavily on the work of the French sociologist, Frederick le Play, who argued that 'good' family organisation was an essential factor contributing to the prosperity and contentment of a people. Where family members developed their sense of responsibility one to the other, Helen Bosanquet (1906, p. 96) argued, 'the Family presented itself as the medium by which the public interest is combined with private welfare'. In this analysis, social problems disappeared when the family was strong and effective; for example, old age pensions were unnecessary 'where the stable Family combines young and old in one strong bond of mutual helpfulness' (Bosanquet, 1906, p. 99). Natural regard for his family's welfare was the primary impetus to the development of the adult male and his becoming a cooperative member of society:

nothing but the considered rights and responsibilities of family life will ever rouse the average man to his full degree of efficiency, and induce him to continue working after he has earned sufficient to meet his own personal needs. The Family in short, is from this point of view, the only known way of ensuring, with any approach to success, that one generation will exert itself in the interests and for the sake of another, and its effect upon the economic efficiency of both generations is in this respect alone of paramount importance. (Ibid., p. 222)

Children also learned the meaning of responsibility and mutual service, trust and affection in their relationships with family members and, because the interests of the child and its pleasures centred on the home, the child naturally wanted to contribute to it. The hallmark of the hopelessly degraded 'residuum' (the Victorian equivalent of the underclass) was lack of family feeling and a failure to socialise the young into 'habits of labour and obedience'.

There was therefore little material aid that could be offered to the family within this framework that would not damage family responsibility and subvert character. The most likely agent to intervene – by offering old age pensions, for example – was the state. State intervention was thus condemned as likely to undermine character, whereas volunteer social workers, suitably trained, would serve to strengthen character and deepen the ties of voluntary obligation within the community. Achieving social change by changing individual habits and will was necessarily an inordinately slow business because the impetus for change had to come from within the individual. Successful change could only take place when the individual was ready for it; it was therefore unlikely that as crude an agent as the state could be effective in securing it. There was also the danger that the state would usurp the individual in the pursuit of his interests, for example by providing school meals for his children, thereby setting back the whole process of true social reform which depended on the individual's struggle to achieve a better life. The final test of any intervention in the life of an individual had to be whether it improved mind and character and it was unlikely that state action would ever be able to pass it. To the COS, both state intervention in the form of material assistance, passed out without due attention to individual circumstance, and the proponents of *laissez-faire* who would leave those in need alone, represented lazy and dangerous approaches to social problems. According to Helen Bosanquet, the real work of charity was therefore 'not to afford facilities [such as material relief] to the poor to lower their standard but to step in when calamity threatened and to prevent it from falling' (H. Bosanquet, 1898, p. 52). Social workers had the responsibility of encouraging poor families to aspire to as high a personal standard in material and cultural terms as possible. Social work needed to combine careful investigation with love and would strive for holistic understanding through the completeness of its casework (B. Bosanquet, 1898).

The practice of social work bore little relation to the ideal. It was not separated from relief, but was in fact often undertaken in order to ascertain whether an applicant was worthy of financial assistance. It is also unlikely that many volunteer social workers knew how to go about the business of changing habits and building character. It was not easy to come to an understanding of the perceptions and motivations of poor families or to work to change these in the absence of any clear methodology. Yet the potential of 'friendly visiting' proved extremely enticing to late nineteenth and early twentieth-century social reformers and by the 1900s the COS stood accused, not of promoting something that was ineffectual, but of not having implemented it properly.

# NOTES

1.  I have taken these leaders of the Society to be representative of the two main strands of opinion within it. I also make reference to the views of others, especially to E.J. Urwick, who was, if anything, more idealist than Loch and Bosanquet, and to Octavia Hill, who occupied something of a middle position, in that, while she had little time for the theory of charity and was passionately convinced by the tenets of classical political economy, she followed the ideas of Loch and Bosanquet in her charitable practice.
2.  Diary of C.S. Loch, 29 September 1888, TS Goldsmiths Library, Senate House, University of London.
3.  See above, p. 10.
4.  Loch, Diary, 14 September 1876.
5.  Ibid., 29 November 1879.
6.  Ibid., 10 September 1888.
7.  Ibid., 1 July 1879.
8.  Beatrice Webb's Diary, 18 May 1883, f. 308, TS. BLPES, LSE.
9.  Loch, Diary, 23 February 1877.
10. Ibid., 29 December 1879.
11. Ibid., 26 July 1879.
12. Octavia Hill to Henrietta Barnett, 26 December 1873, Coll. Misc. 512, BLPES, LSE.
13. Octavia Hill, 'Letter to my Fellow Workers', 1879, p. 6, Coll. D. Misc. 84/5, Marylebone Public Library, London.
14. Loch, Diary, 8 October 1877.
15. Ibid., 17 September 1877.
16. Rev. W.H. Fremantle for St. Mary's Bryanston Sq., *Pastoral Address and Report*

*of the Charities for the year 1870*, supplement to the Report: 'An Attempt to Raise a few of the London Poor without Gifts', letter from John Ruskin, TS, 30 August 1870, BLPES, LSE.

17.  Octavia Hill, 'Letter to my Fellow Workers', 1897, p. 7.
18.  Loch, Diary, 29 December 1879.

# 2.  The practice of charity, 1870–1900

## THE 'HARD AND DRY' YEARS, THE 1870s

The COS was probably at its sternest during the first decade of its existence. The aims of the Society were to increase cooperation with other charities and with the poor law in order to eliminate indiscriminate relief and to uphold the deterrent principles of the poor law; to conduct thorough investigation of applicants for relief before deciding upon a suitable plan of action; to offer material relief only on a temporary basis and where a 'permanent result' might be hoped for; and to repress mendicity. During its early years, the Society was associated strongly with the last of these aims. At the annual general meeting of 1884 it was commented that only one person had referred to the skill of the society in suppressing imposters and that it was 'a kind of triumph that charity and charity organization should have had the first place at the meeting'.[1]

After its widely broadcast enthusiasm to root out those who were begging unnecessarily came the Society's desire to cooperate with the poor law. However, this proved a much more difficult task. The public could be sternly advised not to give alms indiscriminately to beggars, because such relief could only serve further to demoralise and was in the end selfish behaviour, assuaging the conscience of the giver while doing nothing to assist the recipient on a permanent basis. But it was harder to set up policies and procedures that would allow the COS to work alongside the poor law, making sure that only the hopelessly destitute had recourse to statutory relief and establishing some principles for dealing with the rest.

The 1869 Goschen Minute set out a division of labour between the poor law and voluntary action on the basis of client groups, with charity assisting those on the verge of destitution and the poor law acting as the provider of last resort as had been intended in the 1834 reform. Following this, the Local Government Board, which took responsibility for the poor law in 1871, issued a circular instructing the local poor law authorities (the boards of guardians) to tighten up their practices in respect of outdoor relief, especially in regard to those physically capable of working (C. 516, 1872). The COS welcomed this move, seeing it as furthering the idea of a small and deterrent role for the poor law and a large role for charity.

The idea of the 1834 Poor Law Amendment Act had been that applicants for poor relief would have to prove their destitution by their willingness to enter a workhouse in order to get assistance; however, it had never proved possible to end the practice of offering outdoor relief to people living at home. At the end of 1871, the Local Government Board reported that its inquiries showed conclusively that 'out-door relief is in many cases granted by the Guardians too readily and without sufficient inquiry, and that they give it also in numerous instances in which it would be more judicious to apply the workhouse test' (ibid., p. 64). The Board also noted that there was a great diversity of practice in the administration of outdoor relief. It recommended that guardians not grant outdoor relief to single able-bodied men or women, to unmarried mothers, to deserted wives, or to able-bodied widows with more than one child, and that the local relieving officer should visit all recipients of outdoor relief fortnightly. Not all guardians followed the prescriptions of the Board, but the numbers on outdoor relief did fall substantially until the late 1870s (Humphreys, 1991; MacKinnon, 1987; Rose, 1988; Thane, 1978). According to William Chance (1895), a leading member of the London COS, Charity Organisation Society cooperation was vital in securing this reduction. However, outside London the COS was often weak and in any case it experienced considerable difficulties both in securing effective cooperation with local boards of guardians and in working out its own role.

While the Goschen Minute had assigned charity the task of preventing people from becoming a public charge, this left the COS to decide whom to help, and how to help them and, more difficult still, to convince other charities to follow its policy. Initially the Society was anxious not to give any material relief. But what were they to do with an applicant in great need? An early minute of the Council of the London COS recorded the decision that 'when an applicant is truly starving he may be given a piece of bread if he eats it in the presence of the giver'.[2] The information that the COS would not assist someone who was starving before they had been properly investigated travelled fast and was something that the COS was later at pains to deny. At the other extreme, however, it was argued that the COS should pick up the whole task of outdoor relief (albeit with proper investigation of each case), thus ensuring that the role of the poor law was limited to providing assistance in the workhouse.[3] But this threatened to make the COS another relief society, something that Loch was extremely anxious to avoid. As J.R. Holland, a member of the Sub-Committee on Charity and Outrelief, argued, thrift, not charity, was the proper substitute for outdoor relief and it was up to true charity to inculcate the habit of thrift.[4]

Early on in its existence the COS encountered the issues that both served to define its practice and continued to cause it considerable heart-searching. First, it was far from clear how the Society was to differentiate its client group from that of the poor law. Could, for example, the COS help a particular family member if the rest of the family was receiving poor law relief?[5] What was the Society to do with a respectable, elderly couple seeking help, or with a genuinely deserted wife?[6] The answers were various, for the COS was a federal organisation and its local district committees were autonomous in the conduct of their affairs, just as the provincial societies were left free to decide whether to affiliate to the London parent body. The Council of the London COS was convinced that its sphere of operations had to be kept completely separate from that of the poor law. To this end, its committees would thoroughly investigate an applicant and decide whether charitable help was appropriate. It rapidly emerged that the main criterion for such a decision was whether the applicant was deemed to be deserving. On this basis, it was not impossible for any of the cases noted above to be helped. However, the Society did lay down other criteria with regard to the level and form of assistance. It aimed to provide adequate assistance and only to give it in cases where some permanent improvement could be expected. This made 'chronic cases' very difficult to adjudicate. An elderly couple, no matter how deserving, were likely to need continuing assistance. Similarly, a deserted wife with young children was likely to need help for a long time. Initially, it was decided that in such cases the friendly visitor should try to mobilise the support of relatives, or try to put applicants in touch with other charities. However, the pull of doing something for the deserving was strong. In 1875, Octavia Hill reported that in Marylebone the COS committee had stopped giving anything to the single able-bodied and had thus been able to make regular allowances from a small fund to such cases,[7] and in 1878, Sir Charles Trevelyan proposed that the COS make systematic provision for deserving chronic cases.[8]

In deciding to extend its relief function the COS faced the problem of its own lack of funds. An early, rather clumsy attempt to get other charities to agree to a 1 per cent levy in the cause of 'charity organisation' failed (Bosanquet, 1914) and throughout his first decade as general secretary Loch worried constantly about the Society's shaky financial position. This also made it difficult to make sure that relief was adequate. During the early years the Society favoured giving loans to those temporarily unable to work, believing that they were also likely 'to elevate the tone of the poorer classes by inspiring feelings of self-reliance and independence' (COS, 1881); 1039 loans were made in London in 1872. However, defaulting rapidly made the practice less attractive. Most local district committees – there were 40 by the end of the 1880s – went ahead and raised their own relief funds, but they continued to vary considerably in terms of how they related to the poor law authorities and in terms of their own practices.

The COS strove to cooperate closely with other charities particularly church visiting societies, and the poor law, encouraging cross-membership between COS committees and boards of guardians. While the operation of charity and state relief was intended to remain entirely separate, it was thought that such cooperation would ensure that both operated according to a shared set of principles. However, there was relatively little evidence of good cooperation with the machinery of the poor law at the local level. W.A. Bailward (1920) deplored the fact that boards of guardians were elected, complaining that all too often election to the board was viewed as the first step to procuring a paid appointment. In 1878, 24 of 31 COS district committees reported having guardians as members, but in only four London districts was a thoroughly organised system of relief worked out between the COS and the poor law. The position in the provinces was similar. A Society such as the Liverpool Central Relief Society affiliated to the London COS but declared that it would continue to act primarily as a straightforward relief society. Societies explicitly adopting the ideas of the Goschen Minute were rare and, even where cooperation in terms of cross-membership was achieved, as in Oxford, it did not follow that the COS and the guardians cooperated at the level of dealing with individual cases (Humphreys, 1991).

In London, Thomas Mackay (1889) gave special praise to the regime pursued in St George's-in-the-East, where A.G. Crowder, a leading member of the COS, sat as a guardian. The guardians undertook to abolish outdoor relief entirely. Crowder was reported to have attended the relief meetings of the board of guardians, to have entered 'hard cases' in his notebook and to have visited them, finding that no great hardship had been inflicted. Other relatives had come forward to help, some applicants had migrated to laxer districts, and one-third had accepted relief in the workhouse. The work of the guardians was complemented by strict investigation by the COS into the cases coming before them. However, as Sidney and Beatrice Webb (1912) later pointed out, Crowder was not able to do anything to prevent an increase in charitable giving in the form of soup kitchens run by the churches. Indeed, in the work of organising charity, the COS continually complained of lack of cooperation from the parish clergy, who persisted in more traditional forms of district visiting and in the indiscriminate forms of charitable giving that accompanied it. In 1876, Octavia Hill pleaded with the church for 'God's sake' to cooperate in stemming the flood of ruinous doles.[9]

Whitechapel also endeavoured to abolish outdoor relief. Samuel Barnett, a member of the Council of the London COS and founder of Toynbee Hall settlement in 1884, reported that the guardians were happy to send all applicants for outdoor relief to the COS for decision.[10] As a clergyman, Barnett also secured the cooperation of the church. In Barnett's view, the Whitechapel scheme meant

> that the burden of relieving the poor is removed from the shoulders of ratepayers, many of whom can ill-support the burden, all of whom give grudgingly and of necessity. It means also that the poor get the kind of help best fitted to their needs; those only are left to the workhouse for whom it is an asylum or a discipline; those who can be helped by a gift receive the gift without loss of self-respect.[11]

The scheme was thus portrayed as not so much economical as kind. Barnett's ideas about the organisation of relief owed much to the work of Octavia Hill in Marylebone, where he had been a curate before moving to Whitechapel.

Hill's experiment in charity organisation was perhaps the most successful of the 1870s. In Marylebone, she took up the job of secretary to the parish visitors, attending meetings of the parish relief committee as well as the COS committee. All applicants for poor law relief were first passed to the COS committee for investigation and the weeding-out of those not deserving of help. Visitors supplied information on which the decision was based and visited those referred back to the poor law in order to explain matters to them (Hill, 1875). Only in Marylebone did the COS achieve its ideal of a full working cooperation with both the clergy and the poor law authorities. In their *Economics of Industry* (1879), Alfred and Mary Marshall cited Hill's work in support of their arguments regarding state and voluntary aid in poor relief. Hill compared the Marylebone system to the Elberfield scheme in Germany, a much-vaunted model for British administration of relief in the late nineteenth century (Rose, 1981). The appeal of Elberfield for Hill and many others lay in the close personal supervision of each applicant for relief by an unpaid worker who was in fact obliged by law to offer his or her services, a degree of compulsion that did not fit COS philosophy and which Hill conveniently overlooked when citing its merits. The Elberfield workers also had the power to decide the rate of relief to be given, something Hill realised would be impossible until British voluntary workers were better trained, and which would in any case have been virtually impossible to achieve given the well-developed nature of British local administration compared to the German. Hill admitted that on paper the scheme looked 'dry and formal', but she insisted that 'anyone who reflects will see how the most intimate, loving, friendly way of reaching the poor through the efforts of kind visitors (each of whom visits chiefly amongst those she knows best) has been secured' (Hill, 1872, p. 444).

The parameters of the COS's work were in large measure set by the way in which it conceptualised its relationship to the poor law. The Society accepted the principles governing the 1834 reform of the poor law and in its day-to-day practice struggled to bring them closer to reality. In fact, its cooperation with the poor law authorities remained limited, but the focus on the prevention of pauperism meant that, notwithstanding its philosophical commitment to a broad definition of charity as a social principle, the Society became bogged down in establishing the ground rules for giving relief. By the end of the 1870s, the chief preoccupation of the Society was casework and in 1881 paid secretaries were introduced by district committees in order the better to supervise this work. At the beginning of 1882, the Council of the London COS expressed anxiety as to whether the absorption of the COS in casework represented a weakness, but nevertheless went on to consider whether the aims of the Society should not be changed to reflect the focus on the organisation of relief.[12] After all, the organisation of the individual case could be defended as the basis of good organisation in a district. Loch pointed out that, while the more careful the casework the more the 'time and strength' of district committee were monopolised by it, 'those who care for helping the poor will not cooperate on a theory; their confidence will only be won by the work of the Society being better on every point – not merely in investigation, but in personal care, etc. – than the work of other agencies'.[13] In addition, given the great importance attached by idealists in the Society to the importance of changing individual habits, the practice of sound casework acquired a particular importance. Bernard Bosanquet had no problem with the fact that casework had come to predominate in the work of the COS and had 'in some degree put out of sight the direct campaign of organisation of charities and reform of poor law administration' (Bosanquet, 1898, p. 129). But his view was premised on the assumption that good casework did not automatically mean relief work, but rather emphasised educational work with poor families. However, it was hard to convince either recipients or outside observers that what the COS considered to be good casework was not harsh.

The story of the 'Peek gift' is a good case in point. Mr Francis Peek was a member of the COS and of the London School Board between 1873 and 1874, and in 1875 he made available £1000 a year for the relief of cases of distress that emerged in the course of the work of school board committees considering the cases of parents who had failed to pay their children's school fees. The 1870 Education Act set up local school boards and obliged them to make sure that sufficient places were available for all children of elementary school age; it also permitted the boards to remit the fees of pupils in their own schools and to pay the fees of poor children attending voluntary schools. The London School Board made its work particularly hard by opting for both compulsory school attendance and a fee-paying system; the latter was not abandoned until 1890 (Lewis, 1982; Rubinstein, 1969). Any child one week in arrears with fees was excluded from school and the parents were asked to come before the divisional committees of the board to present their reasons for non-payment; if remission was refused the parents were summonsed to appear before a magistrate. The fees in London schools ranged from 1d to 9d per week, ensuring some automatic separation of the respectable from the non-respectable poor. But the school board agonised over remitting or paying fees on behalf of poor children because of the fear that their families would thereby be pauperised. Widespread remission or payment was bound to threaten the structure of the poor law because it amounted to a species of outdoor relief. Certainly, the COS believed that parents who could not pay school fees must by definition be paupers and should therefore go to the guardians for relief, not the school board.[14] It feared too that free education offered a premium on parental neglect and could only lead to a call for free breakfasts and free clothes. Free education could only lead to yet more state intervention and the wholesale assumption of what were crucially considered to be parental responsibilities.

In the view of the COS, the divisional committees of the board were making decisions about the remission or payment of fees after only cursory investigation. The Society considered it very important that only the deserving among those being considered for remission or payment should be assisted. The undeserving should be forced to resort to the poor law or be summonsed to appear before the magistrates. Ideally, the COS would have liked to establish systematic cooperation with the board, whereby it submitted all cases to the Society's workers before coming to a decision, but only the Westminster Division of the board obliged in this respect.[15] In fact, the evidence suggests that the school board took its decisions over remission or payment very seriously indeed. Thus remittance for a chronically unemployed shoemaker was delayed a week while the board asked its visitor to inquire why a shoemaker should have difficulty in finding work and, in the case of an unemployed painter, it was judged a point in his favour that he had tried to support his family by 'parting with his things' (Lewis, 1982, p. 298).

Nevertheless, the COS viewed the administration of the 'Peek gift' as an opportunity to encourage the board to separate the deserving from the undeserving. The board's visitors were to cooperate with the COS in investigating cases of distress. Help would be offered from the Peek fund to those families where there was the prospect of long-term improvement. However, in 1877, the superintendents of the school board's visitors wrote to Mr Peek to ask 'that each case should be considered solely upon its merits and that the amount needed for relief should be decided with reference to the interests of the child in the first place and secondly with a view to the general benefit of the family'.[16] They also requested that special consideration be given deserted wives and widows, the able-bodied who were temporarily out of work and families with large numbers of young children, expressing the opinion that boots (always a major item of expenditure for poor families) and clothing would make particularly appropriate gifts in the majority of cases. In reply, the COS patiently explained its philosophy. In the first place the cause of distress needed to be established and only then could relief be given sufficient to ensure permanent improvement. If the cause of distress was drunkenness or idleness on the part of the parent, then no relief could be given. The needs of the child could not be considered in isolation from the rest of the family. Even if the family was deserving, a gift of boots would not ensure permanent improvement and would in all probability contribute to further demoralisation. In sum, 'relief which made the parents improvident would not be, in the long run, beneficial to the child'.[17] The COS argued that, if it were widely known that the Peek fund would provide boots on request, then parents might well keep their children at home in order to get boots, thus further frustrating the work of the board. As for giving special consideration to deserted wives and to widows, recourse to the poor law and the workhouse was usually necessary in these cases because the women's earnings would rarely ever prove sufficient in the long term. Nor could temporary unemployment or large families in and of themselves constitute sufficient grounds for relief; the applicants should also have demonstrated thrift and a willingness to help themselves.

Until the Peek fund expired in 1884, the school board visitors and the chairman of the board continued to plead for greater liberality in its administration on the grounds that, while not all cases might be wholly deserving, 'it should be borne in mind that if children could be got into regular attendance in school they acquired habits of punctuality, order and discipline, and this would tend to bring them above the level of pauperism'.[18] The COS accepted the positive value of education, but persisted in regarding the gift of boots or clothing as supremely dangerous. From the school board's point of view, the problem was that the COS's policy of granting assistance only to the deserving poor clashed with the board's desire to get all children into school and in particular the children of parents who were idle and vicious. The fact that the arguments of the board's visitors made little impression on the Society showed the strength of the COS's faith in its analysis of the importance of family responsibility in fostering character. But its ideas were never accepted by the school board visitors and its practice was deemed harsh by this group and by many others. During the early 1880s the Peek fund degenerated into a 'boots fund' under pressure from the school board officials, until in 1884 Mr Peek abandoned his experiment.

## CRITICISM FROM WITHIN AND WITHOUT, 1870–1900

The problems the COS experienced in administering the Peek gift reflected the larger problems the Society was having in classifying the poor. As early as 1874, W.E. Forster, head of the Education Department in the Liberal government of the early 1870s, took the chair for the

COS's annual general meeting and assured those present that the Society was not guided by strict and rigid principles of political economy, confining relief only to the deserving.[19] However, that was precisely what many district committees were striving to do, however unsuccessfully. The COS classified applicants for relief into those who were assisted, those who were not assisted and those who were referred elsewhere. However, the 'not assisted' comprised two main groups: the undeserving and the ineligible. The COS remained firm on the question of the undeserving: they could not be helped and had to go to the poor law. However, the ineligibles were not necessarily undeserving, but rather might need the kind of long-term help that the COS could not give. Thus those categorised as 'ineligible' threatened to undermine the distinction between the deserving and the undeserving. In 1878, the District Committee of St. George's Hanover Square reported that far too many deserving cases were being written off as ineligible because the Committee lacked the resources to help them:

> When the Society first came into existence it was calculated that the charitable funds of London were sufficient to maintain every eighth person in comfort. Theory, however, in this instance, as in many more, has to yield to fact; and your Committee find that, until the stream of charity can be conducted into truer channels, the stubborn fact meets them that the proper local agency or private person cannot at a moment's notice be found to meet the pressing emergency.[20]

In fact, during the 1870s, the London COS assisted only about one-third of applicants, relatively few compared to the provincial societies (Humphreys, 1991). In 1883, the *Charity Organisation Reporter* commented gloomily that, despite the successful abolition of outdoor relief in Stepney, St. Georges-in-the-East and Whitechapel, as a result of the cooperation between the COS and the poor law and the benefit that had accrued to the ratepayers, those same ratepayers had not seen fit to contribute to the charity that had made it all possible.[21]

The problem of the unassisted 'ineligibles' also threatened to undermine the whole *raison d'être* for friendly visiting within the Society. Beatrice Webb struggled with the problem of those deemed to be ineligible for help during the period she spent as a rent collector. A tenant who was out of work because of sickness, unable to pay his rent and therefore facing eviction and the poor law could not be assisted by the COS because he needed long-term help, but, as Webb noted, the deserving were all too often those whom it was impossible to help effectively within the framework of COS principles. And, as she further noted, it was difficult to see how such principles could be 'made consistent with the duty persistently inculcated of personal friendship with the poor' (Webb, 1926, p. 102). In 1884, Henrietta Barnett, who had been a rent collector for Octavia Hill before her marriage to Samuel Barnett, charged the COS with lacking a large enough heart. An applicant might be ineligible for relief, but surely not for charitable effort (Barnett, 1884). Similarly, Margaret Sewell, also a close friend of Octavia Hill's, who became head worker at the Women's University Settlement in 1891, was convinced that some kind of help should be offered those deemed ineligible for relief. Sewell felt that the tendency of the COS to leave those who could not be helped by money to their own devices lost it public sympathy.[22] It was also the case that COS practice of leaving 'ineligibles' to their fate was severely at odds with the COS theory of visiting.

This gap between theory and practice existed even in the case of those who might be classified as undeserving, as Octavia Hill recognised:

> A man comes up and the Committee decides to do nothing, he ought to save, an elder lad ought to go to work, he ought to send some child to a hospital. Nothing to be done! No nothing by the Committee perhaps, nothing definite at a given time by the visitor, but refusal can hardly be a help to the man unless it is again and again gently explained, unless advice is given, information procured.[23]

The COS ran the risk of not getting to 'know' the poor as it should. In 1877, Hill wrote: 'The COS is suffering grievously at its centre; the tone gets harder, the alienation deeper. They ought to be brought into close contact with the workers among the poor.'[24] Hill felt that the district committees of the COS, composed mainly of men, were too removed from the poor.

Octavia Hill was not alone in her concern about the lack of sympathy in COS offices and about the whole procedure of investigation. In his diary, Loch reiterated his belief that it could not be better to offer relief to 12 men without proper investigation than to pass by one deserving person, what he termed the '12 to 1 fallacy'.[25] But he also worried about the evidence of inefficiency, 'pettishness' and harshness in the districts.[26] During the early 1880s, concern was frequently expressed about the work of the paid agents in the districts. These were often ex-servicemen or policemen with no experience of casework, who were used to take case histories ('take down a case' in COS parlance). In Bradford, the legendary harshness of the paid agent was a contributing factor in the setting up of a rival organisation to the COS in the form of the Bradford City Guild of Help (Cahill and Jowitt, 1980). The Society would have liked to attract a higher class of agent, but was unable to do so for the money it offered. Its district secretaries tended to be of the middle class, but many of these were female.

In 1882, it was suggested that it would be best if a voluntary committee member took responsibility for each applicant to ensure proper treatment: 'Personal care is at the root of our work.'[27] It was above all important for an applicant to feel that he was helped sympathetically. In an editorial in 1883, the *Charity Organisation Reporter* asked its readers to consider the case of a woman coming to a COS office to apply for relief: 'She has to wait for some time, in company with others, in a room absolutely bare of anything that can interest her. She then goes into another room, where she is asked and answers a good many questions, and she departs.' After some time she might be told to come to the office again to collect the assistance she asked for. 'Very likely the agent of a member of the Committee has called in the meantime and had a pleasant and sympathetic talk with her', but the clergyman or district visitor would have done as much if she had applied to the vestry. Because the COS was a Society for organising charitable relief and not a mere relieving Society, there was 'less excuse for the absence of humanity in charity'. It was suggested that applicants should be able to come to a COS office for a friendly discussion as to the nature of their distress, just as a patient attended the doctor's surgery not solely for medicine but for consultation on how to recover health.[28] The Honorary Secretary of the Hackney COS, N. Masterman, who was in the 1900s to transfer his allegiance to the rival personal service societies, the guilds of help, also hammered home the need for more 'feeling' in the work of the offices of the COS during the 1880s (Masterman, 1885). It is important to note that neither Masterman nor Hill was in favour of a more lenient policy towards outdoor relief; their criticism consisted entirely of the way in which the society was conducting its casework.

Aware of these criticisms, the COS changed the nature of its classification of applicants several times during the 1880s and 1890s. In 1886, the 'undeserving' became those 'not likely to benefit' from assistance. However, it proved difficult to banish the concept of the undeserving from COS thinking and, in 1893, Helen Bosanquet addressed the issue of classification again. Echoing Beatrice Webb a decade before, she asked, 'how many of us would have been more deserving under the circumstances?' and recommended that the Society confine itself to distinguishing between the 'helpable' and the 'unhelpable'. However, she was careful to justify such a distinction in moral terms, while the Society would no longer have to play moral arbiter, separating the deserving sheep from the undeserving goats, nor would applicants be tempted to pretend to be something that they were not: 'We will not use our charity as a reward of merit; if we do we shall only foster hypocrisy and deceit...' (H. Bosanquet, 1893, p. 209). The category of 'helpable' would, she felt, focus the social worker's mind firmly on the need for good investigation to discover the real cause of poverty and then act. A man listed as being 'out of work through no fault of his own' had no meaning; there was always a reason for unemployment, by which she meant a failure of character.

Bosanquet's approach was reiterated in the papers the COS published during the 1890s in an effort to guide district committees towards sounder casework practice. H.L. Woollcombe (1893), who was appointed to the new post of organising secretary in 1898 (designed to oversee the practice of the district committees), emphasised that the object of investigation was not to sift out the undeserving. It was impossible to arrive at a scientific measure of desert and in any case, the undeserving might well be more in need of true charitable attention. Nevertheless, it is hard to avoid the conclusion that these changes were largely cosmetic. The COS continued to refine its casework practice, recording family history, employment history, details of living conditions and rent, debts, previous relief history and club memberships, and seeking character references for all applicants. But after due process of investigation it invariably decided that it could not help in cases of 'slackness of work', that is in cases of underemployment and low income, which the social investigations of Booth and Rowntree showed to be the main cause of poverty in the late Victorian period. Helen Bosanquet (1898) advised that in cases of 'insufficient income' emigration should be suggested, or efforts made to get children into the labour force.

The Society did try harder to help 'chronic cases', mainly the respectable elderly poor. Octavia Hill consistently sought donors for the provision of adequate pensions for this group and became increasingly angry at the difficulty COS committees experienced in raising subscriptions for the provision of pensions (Hill, 1898). The idea of state pensions began to be discussed during the 1880s and 1890s; Booth became an advocate of a state scheme because his survey of London showed old age to be such a significant cause of poverty. The COS was therefore anxious to show that the needs of the elderly could be met by charity and during the 1890s district committees were encouraged to raise funds on an individual case-by-case basis after investigation.[29] But the COS was never able to show that its individual casework method could be effectively employed for the purposes of relief; the numbers in need were too great and the COS's efforts were too patchy, poorly funded and insufficiently staffed.

Bernard Bosanquet had admitted that personal social service demanded 'armies' of volunteer visitors. But these were never forthcoming. Nor were staff especially well-versed in the methods of casework, on which so much had come to depend by the 1880s. The Society accepted the need for paid district secretaries in addition to paid agents in 1881, and by the end of the 1880s half these were women, who, despite repeated calls for equal remuneration, were paid considerably less than the men. When Helen Dendy (later Bosanquet) was appointed in 1890, she was paid £80 a year, whereas E.J. Urwick was given £100 in 1893. Loch (1903) was concerned that by 1900 so much of the work of the Society rested in the hands of women, fearing that unless men were prepared to get more involved the status and influence of the COS would be adversely affected. Nevertheless, the principle of voluntary personal social service occupied an important place in the philosophy of the COS and was strongly defended during the 1890s. Two prominent members of the Society, Mr and Mrs Dunn-Gardner, resigned over the appointment of a paid secretary in Lambeth, preferring a scheme whereby volunteers would receive training (Dunn-Gardner, 1895). The appointment of paid secretaries continued, supplemented by organising secretaries who paid special attention to levels of training in the districts and the ways in which district offices were organised, but in addition the Society began training courses for volunteers in 1897, in conjunction with the Women's University Settlement.

The experience of the average COS volunteer visitor is hard to capture. Leaders of the Society repeatedly expressed their concern that volunteers were not well treated when they appeared in COS offices. They were often given too many routine tasks, such as copying letters asking other charities to help a particular applicant, and were denied access by paid secretaries to the case papers that would have piqued their interest. District visitors, with whom the COS ideally wished to establish better cooperation, also tended to find themselves snubbed.[30]

A.L. Hodson, a young woman settlement worker at the turn of the century, recorded her experiences visiting for the COS. She had wanted to go to Oxford, but her father opposed this and a compromise was reached in the form of voluntary work at a settlement. She found the dirt and noise of the neighbourhood trying. She did not like visiting after dark or on Mondays when the 'nicer people are all out, and among the nasty ones I do not like to see fighting and drunkenness' (Hodson, 1909, p. 136). She also found it very difficult to follow COS principles: 'The unfortunate part of it is, that I find it so very difficult to apply the theories of relief, as taught by the COS, to any of the practical cases I come across.' She agreed that most of her cases exhibited failures of character and that money was therefore not the answer. However, she was unsure as to how then to proceed, finding COS ideas 'interesting, generally convincing, but a little paralysing' (ibid., p. 22). She found taking down a case difficult: 'To sit opposite a proud, sensitive man and be obliged to ask him all sorts of questions about his family, his work, his income, and debts, makes me feel hot and cold all over' (ibid., p. 30). Hodson also worked as a district visitor for her parish, which she disliked because she hated to call on people when there was no reason. At the meetings of the district visitors she sat as both a district visitor and a representative of the COS, which posed difficulties because district visitors hated the COS, regarding its principles as 'impossible and undenominational' (ibid., p. 137). There is every reason to suppose that Hodson's experience was quite typical. After thorough investigation, the COS had only limited amounts of money to give. And if money was not given, it is likely that the vast majority of its social workers were uncertain as to how to go on to build character. Even the very small number who attended the lecture series mounted by the Society at the Women's University Settlement and later at its own School of Sociology would have received no instruction in the methods of casework, the courses being entirely focused on principles and social theory. This uncertainty regarding the practice of social work, as well as lack of manpower, helps to explain why so little was done for the vast majority of applicants who fell into the category of 'not-assisted'.

The late nineteenth and very early twentieth century is usually regarded as the period during which the COS was at its most confident and influential, yet the Society was struggling with fundamental issues of procedure and purpose. Loch himself was far from content with the way in which the Society was conducting itself. In a private memorandum circulated to members of the Society in 1885, he confessed that he felt unable to encourage people to join the COS as it stood. He had not joined the Society to cooperate with the poor law, to secure proper investigation of applicants for relief, or to repress mendicity, but for the larger purpose of improving the condition of the poor. As it was, he believed that the COS was seen as a middle-class society that administered relief by an expensive method and by proxy. Loch reiterated his view that charity organisation had to mean more than the simple organisation of relief. More attention had to be paid to organising the work of charitable agencies and the poor law, but also to the work of visiting. All too often a paid agent took down a case, the committee reached a decision, but no 'friend' was forthcoming. In so far as relief was the business of district committees it had to be regulated, not by deterrent methods, but by knowledge. Ideally, Loch would have liked to give the Society a new name: The Society for Friendly and Associated Charity (Loch, 1885).

In many respects Loch's list of problems summarised the internal debates of the Society during the last two decades of the nineteenth century. At the same time, the Society was beginning to face what it perceived as growing external threats, particularly from the state. Following the severe unemployment of the mid-1880s and the social unrest that accompanied it, the government issued the Chamberlain Circular in 1886, which urged local authorities to schedule public works for periods of depression and to cooperate with the poor law guardians in providing temporary, non-pauperising employment for the deserving. This was anathema to the COS, as was the hurried charitable response in raising a Mansion House Fund, which the COS condemned as a vast outpouring of indiscriminate relief. The Society spoke up for casework methods in dealing with the unemployed, but between 1886 and 1896 it assisted only some 800 cases a year to find work. The numbers out of work in 1886 were recognised by the Society to be beyond the reach of philanthropy, but it continued to recommend education and the development of the habit of thrift as the best remedies. Yet, as José Harris (1972) has pointed out, the COS was in the end less concerned with either promoting the idea of self-sufficiency or with denying the economic fact of unemployment than with keeping the treatment of the problem under its control. While disapproving of the Mansion House committees, Loch played a prominent role in arranging relief in the form of employment for them. On the other hand, he condemned the Toynbee Hall Conference which proposed an almost identical relief scheme in conjunction with the local vestries and the London County Council, the difference being that this scheme recommended the provision of work by the local authorities. The COS struggled to make sure that any scheme came under wise, *voluntary* management in which it played a dominant part.

This pattern was to be repeated. Any proposed incursion of the state into the realm of social reform (other than in respect of the 'feeble-minded', who by the end of the nineteenth century were regarded as a threat to racial progress by a wide range of political opinion) was fiercely resisted as an incursion into what the COS regarded, for philosophical as well as pragmatic reasons, as the territory of charity. However, if, as repeatedly happened, the COS lost ground, it made every effort to influence the new arrangements as best it could. The COS's continuing campaign against state aid to children provides a good example of this. From the mid-1880s, the campaign to remit the school fees of children was accompanied by a campaign to provide free school dinners. The debate about the problem of undernourished school children began with the 'overpressure' debate, which revolved around the question of whether children were not too ill-fed to profit from compulsory education. From the first, the COS opposed free food for children, using many of the same arguments that it used in the debate over the remission of fees: the child could not be treated in isolation from the parents for fear of undermining parental responsibility, nor would any treatment be successful if the real problem was parental neglect.[31] The COS saw evidence in the new campaign of all that it feared most. By 1891, free education was a fact and free food looked set to follow. Such demoralisation of the family as the fundamental social unit was bound to have severe repurcussions for the health and welfare of the nation as a whole. The Society was determined to hold the line on this issue and set up a special committee to consider the problem. Not surprisingly, it recommended that it was undesirable to create any new machinery for the purpose of school feeding and that it was best to arrange a supply of food to the few who needed it under the auspices of charity using the casework method (COS, 1891).

However, in 1889, the London School Dinners Association was formed. It estimated that between 25 000 and 60 000 school children needed meals and launched an appeal for funds. The COS proposed an alternative to any school board manager who was sympathetic: the COS would undertake to investigate all children said by teachers to be in need of feeding. In the limited number of schools that were prepared to cooperate with it, the Society found large numbers of children not to be in need of aid at all. In cases where the children came from destitute families, then it was proper for the whole family to be relieved by the poor law. Where the parents were negligent, it was preferable to do nothing at all: 'it is better, in the interests of the community, to allow in such cases the sins of the parents to be visited on their children than to impair the principle of the solidarity of the family' (COS, 1893, p.18). Only in cases where the parents were temporarily unable to provide for their children was there a case for providing school meals, and charity was well able to cope with these cases. Loch (1910) stressed the temptation school meals posed to mothers to neglect their children's welfare, but Helen Bosanquet and other women social investigators felt that the real danger was to the more fragile male incentive to provide. In *The Family*, Bosanquet quoted a woman who said that she was glad that there had been no school feeding when her children were at school because her husband spent too much on drink and would have cut her slender housekeeping money further had state meals been available (Bosanquet, 1906, p.313).

In a lecture delivered to the London COS in 1901, Bernard Bosanquet neatly summarised the reasons why the Society felt it had to oppose free school meals:

> Society is naturally self-supporting. The individual and the family, as well for their own good as for the common good, should provide themselves with the necessaries of maintenance, by their own exertions and out of their own resources. If the state undertakes this provision it cannot justify its action on the ground that by so doing it enables the individual to develop his powers or turns to account for the good of the family and the community forces that would otherwise have been lost or wasted. The result is the very reverse of this. By such action the motive for a sound and well-ordered family life is weakened, and a kind of education, the most important to the individual and the State, the education of the child within the family, is discountenanced and hampered.
>
> By a law of social development, then, the individual and the family under normal conditions have to maintain themselves by the exercise of personal energy and mutual aid; and only on these terms are they competent to render the best service to the community. It should therefore be the chief aim of social effort to help the individual to maintain himself throughout life, and to strengthen the sense of obligation and affection which is inherent in the family. All legislation or voluntary action that has a social purpose should be judged by this standard. It is right or wrong as it promotes or frustrates this aim.[32]

However, as Bosanquet acknowledged, it was hard for COS theory to compete with the promise of immediate gratification held out by competing voluntary agencies and, increasingly, by the state. The majority of members of the COS would have agreed with Joseph Lee, when he described the Society's opposition to school meals as a crucial last stand: 'outlying territory we can abandon, but here our citadel is reached. If we cannot defend this wall we might as well surrender'.[33]

However, when the government passed the 1906 Education (Provision of Meals) Act, which permitted local authorities to raise a rate for the purpose of providing school meals, the Society immediately set out to make the best of a bad job. The school meals Act was followed in 1907 by the Education (Administrative Provisions) Act making it a statutory duty for all local authorities medically to examine (but not to treat) all school children. In London the London County Council (LCC) decided to fulfil its obligations under the two pieces of legislation by working through voluntary 'care committees', whose members visited the homes of children recommended for school meals and interviewed mothers after their children were medically inspected (Jennings, 1930). Loch saw the care committees as the only hopeful outcome of the legislation and it immediately became the aim of the COS to gain as much control over them as possible. However, even when the COS did establish control over a particular committee, it was not able to operate entirely as it would have wished. The Reverend Henry Iselin reported that, in respect of cases recommended for meals, his East London committee did not have time for proper investigation and was unable to pursue alternative methods of treatment for particular cases because the law obliged them to feed 'the supposedly underfed' child. But the committee was able to ensure that 'the food was distributed at such an hour and was of such a character as to constitute in itself a definite test of need' (Iselin, 1912, p. 43). The Council of the COS recommended that committees only give children porridge and milk because poor parents did not greatly value these foods. They also strove to maintain some parental involvement, insisting that parents should at least apply for the food on behalf of their children in writing.[34] However, many committees saw their work in very different terms and were inclined to act preventively, feeding children from poor families before any signs of physical malnutrition were apparent (Jennings, 1930). The care committees represented a substantial voluntary/statutory partnership, involving some 12 000 volunteers.[35] The scale and nature of the cooperation were new. To some extent the COS's stress on casework received recognition in the operation of the care committees, which it did not in respect of other social reforms, for example those concerning the unemployed, whose numbers were too great to permit casework. But the local authority rather than the COS controlled the development of care committees. Indeed, in terms of its form, the care committee form was much more like inter-war developments in statutory/voluntary relations, which the COS also accepted with bad grace. With school meals, as with old age pensions and national insurance, the stand taken by the COS was perceived as reactionary.

The COS was also the target of criticism from influential individuals during the late nineteenth century. Samuel Barnett and Alfred Marshall attacked the Society for the rigidity of its principles and suggested that it needed to revise its ideas regarding the boundary between voluntary and state action. In an attack on Marshall's arguments for old age pensions, Bernard Bosanquet defended the 1869 formulation of the divisions between charity and the poor law based, in his view, on the fact that the poor law took the 'hopeless' (undeserving) cases, where there was no sign of the possibility of a return to self-maintenance, and charity the more complicated (deserving) cases, where there were 'points' of character or capacity (Bosanquet, 1892). In reply, Marshall stated, first, that he had no rooted objection to outdoor relief, which he did not believe would necessarily lower wages as the COS continued to argue it must, and in fact looked forward to the time when the poor law would be abolished and 'higher forms' of aid for the working classes introduced (he gave evidence to the 1895 Royal Commission on the Aged Poor in favour of old age pensions). In the meantime, he urged COS committees to work with the poor law in the sense of becoming 'semi-official bodies ... perhaps receiving on their Committees some working men and women representatives of the Local Authority, and having in return the power to nominate some Poor-law Guardians' (Marshall, 1892, p. 378). Marshall thus envisaged joint machinery as well as joint working between the COS and the poor law premised on the abandonment of a fiercely deterrent poor law and the firm division between poor law and charity clients. Thomas Mackay was able to join Bosanquet in defending the position of the COS against such suggestions for root and branch reform, arguing firmly for the poor law as a destitution authority providing indoor relief and the COS as an organisation giving adequate relief to those likely to reap permanent benefit. In his view, Marshall's proposals could only prove 'fatal' to the usefulness of the COS (Mackay, 1896, p. 279).

In his 'friendly criticism' of the COS, Samuel Barnett also accepted that forms of state aid to working people, such as old age pensions, were desirable (Barnett, 1895). As early as 1883, he began to explore the idea that the state should meet men's needs, defined as things that are 'good', but which men did not necessarily recognise to be such (for example, education), while the people supplied their own wants, defined in terms of things they recognised as necessary for life, such as food and clothing. Thus the 'means of life' would be provided by the state, while citizens would have to work for the 'means of livelihood' (Barnett and Barnett, 1894, pp. 244–5). Barnett admitted that these principles were too difficult to define to provide a good guide to the limits of state action. But, like Marshall, he had abandoned the idea that all forms of help outside the workhouse were wrong. By the late 1880s, he was prepared to put training for the unemployed in the hands of the state rather than of charity. Barnett saw the possibility for an expansion of the role of the state, whereupon the rationale for a firm division of labour between charity and the poor law based on the division of the poor into the helpable and unhelpable also disappeared. But he remained opposed to outdoor relief under the poor law, envisaging that the harsh treatment of 'loafers' would become easier once provision was made for needs (ibid., p. 108). Nevertheless, he wanted the COS to cooperate more with the state, for example by visiting poor law cases and the families of board school children who required school meals.

Barnett's criticism was inspired by his observation that notwithstanding the efforts of the COS, the poor remained miserable. Like Henrietta Barnett almost a decade before, he called on the COS to abandon dogmatic principles. Loch had also confessed himself to be worried about the COS's apparent lack of success in improving the condition of the poor, but he could not bring himself to accept the idea of a reconfiguration of the boundary between the statutory and the voluntary sector, especially when it involved a larger role for the state. He treated Barnett's criticism as a personal attack and accused him of bending with the wind, lending his support to socialists who would municipalise everything (Loch, 1895). The Society's participation in the care committees formed after 1907 effectively brought into being the kind of cooperation that Barnett wanted to see in 1895. But the COS persisted in fighting a rearguard action. It never became reconciled to either the new liberalism of the early twentieth century or the new mechanisms developed by the state for delivering social provision.

But in the early decades of the twentieth century it had to face competition from new personal service societies – the councils of social service and guilds of help – set up explicitly to challenge the methods of the COS and to modify its principles, particularly in respect of the distinction it drew between helpable charity clients and unhelpable poor law clients.

## NOTES

1. 'The Annual Meeting', *Charity Organisation Reporter*, 31 May 1884, p. 173.
2. FWA Council Minutes, 17 January 1870, A/FWA/C/A1/1, f. 115, FWA Papers, Greater London Record Office.
3. 'Proceedings of Council', *Charity Organisation Reporter*, 3 May 1876, p. 52.
4. 'Report of the Sub-Committee on Charity and Outrelief', *Charity Organisation Reporter*, 17 May 1877, pp. 88–9
5. 'Proceedings of Council', *Charity Organisation Reporter*, 26 January 1876, p. 17.
6. 'Chronic Cases of Distress', *Charity Organisation Reporter*, 15 January 1873, p. 5; 'Proceedings of Council', ibid., 26 May 1875, p. 77.
7. 'Proceedings of Council', *Charity Organisation Reporter*, 12 May 1875, p. 73.
8. 'Chronic Cases', *Charity Organisation Reporter*, 7 March 1878, p. 45.
9. Octavia Hill, 'Letter to my Fellow Workers', 1876, p. 12, D. Misc. 84/5, Marylebone Public Library, London.
10. 'Report of a Conference on Charity Organisation', *Charity Organisation Reporter*, 1 July 1880, p. 161.
11. 'Charity Organisation and Church Agencies', *Charity Organisation Reporter*, 13 January 1881, p. 13.
12. 'Name and Objects of the Society', *Charity Organisation Reporter*, 2 February 1882, pp. 30–31.
13. 'Secretary's Report on visits to District Committees', *Charity Organisation Reporter*, 9 February 1882, p. 40.
14. 'Proceedings of Council', *Charity Organisation Reporter*, 27 March 1872, p. 54.
15. 'Proceedings of Council', *Charity Organisation Reporter*, 2 April 1873, p. 57.
16. Letter from the Superintendents of Visitors to Mr Francis Peek, dated 20 October 1877, *Charity Organisation Reporter*, 11 July 1878, p. 132.
17. Reply of the Council, dated 1 April 1878, ibid., p. 133.
18. 'Annual Meeting of the COS', address by the Chairman of the London School Board, *Charity Organisation Reporter*, 11 May 1882, p. 139.
19. 'Annual General Meeting', *Charity Organisation Reporter*, 25 March 1874, p. 230.
20. 'Adequate Relief', *Charity Organisation Reporter*, 31 January 1878, p. 21.
21. 'An Experiment in Danger', *Charity Organisation Reporter*, 6 September 1883, p. 273.
22. Margaret Sewell, 'Some Aspects of Charity Organisation', 29 November 1897, A/FWA/C/A1/11/1, f. 288.
23. Octavia Hill to Rev. Fremantle, 1 November 1874, Coll. Misc. 512, BPLES, LSE.
24. Octavia Hill, 'Letter to My Fellow Workers, 1877', p. 10.
25. C.S. Loch, Diary, 28 May 1877, Goldsmith's Library, Senate House, University of London.
26. Ibid., 17 April 1877 and 30 November 1877.
27. 'Applicants in the Office', *Charity Organisation Reporter*, 9 March 1882, p. 63.

28.  'Charity and Humanity', *Charity Organisation Reporter*, 5 July 1883, p. 217.
29.  Report of the Districts Sub-Committee on the Relief Work of the Society, 18 November 1901, A/FWA/C/A1/12.
30.  'District Visitors and the COS', *Charity Organisation Review*, February 1888, p. 70.
31.  'Food and Clothing for School Children', *Charity Organisation Reporter*, 6 December 1883, p. 363.
32.  Bernard Bosanquet, 'Lectures on Charitable and Social Work', 15 April 1901, A/FWA/C/A3/38/1, f. 123.
33.  Joseph Lee, 'The Integrity of the Family: A Vital Issue', COS Report (n.d.), Bosanquet Papers, Trunk II, Box H, University of Newcastle Library.
34.  'The Provision of Meals in Connection with Children's (School) Care Committees', 12 June 1911, A/FWA/ C/A1/14/1, f. 203.
35.  R. Blair to Cyril Jackson, n.d., EO/WEL/1/1, Greater London Record Office.

# 3. The COS and new forms of charity organisation, 1900–1918

The councils of social welfare and guilds of help that were founded in the 1900s and 1910s shared the COS's conviction as to the importance of the role of charity and voluntary action, but were less inclined to propound a theory of charity than to promote ideas regarding its practice. While they were very critical of the COS, their ideas were in many respects very similar, especially in regard to the importance they attached to friendly visiting. However, the new organisations did appear to be different. In large measure it was a matter of attitude rather than actual day-to-day practice. The guilds and councils stressed their civic ideals: they were there to serve everyone. As part of this more positive approach, they were also prepared both to countenance state intervention in the field of social welfare and to cooperate in a different way with the state. Thus, while the new organisations were not so dissimilar from the COS in the work they did, their idea of the relationship between the statutory and voluntary sectors served fundamentally to undermine the firm boundary between the two set up by the COS. The COS continued to exercise considerable influence, particularly during the 1900s, as its strong presence on the Royal Commission appointed in 1905 to look at the poor laws demonstrated, but the views of the guilds and the councils about the terms of voluntary/statutory cooperation and about the practice of casework rapidly gained prominence.

Samuel Barnett became the chairman of the Stepney Council of Social Welfare in 1903. One of his admirers, Thomas Hancock-Nunn, who was a member of the Stepney Board of Guardians and the London County Council and who also had served as an assistant to Ben Tillett during the 1889 dock strike, went on to found a similar organisation in Hampstead. He held this up as a new model for charity organisation in a Memorandum he wrote for the 1909 Report of the Royal Commission on the Poor Laws (of which he was a member). Hancock-Nunn always claimed adherence to the principles of the COS, by which he probably meant a commitment to the idea of reciprocity and a faith in dealing with individuals. He remained on good terms with Loch, who described him to Urwick as 'a white-souled man' (Anon., 1942, p.75). However, Hancock-Nunn was fiercely critical of the COS for abandoning the task of organising a district. In his view, the COS had turned into a relief society that gave too little and a detective agency that inquired too much (Hancock-Nunn, 1909).

By 1914, Hancock-Nunn and D'Aeth, the first secretary of the Liverpool Council of Voluntary Aid (which became the Liverpool Council of Social Service) were identifying the councils and guilds as separate organisational forms, the councils focusing more on securing cooperation within a district and the guilds on personal social work (D'Aeth, 1914). But in the 1900s, Hancock-Nunn's council of social welfare in Hampstead also organised visiting. Any particular district would usually have only one form of organisation and in Hampstead the council absorbed the local COS, just as did many of the guilds in the north of England. The guilds grew fast, especially outside London. By 1911, there were 60 of them with a membership of 8000, which surpassed that of the COS (Cd 5664).

Hancock-Nunn described cooperation as the driving idea behind his council of social welfare. He dismissed the kind of relationship that the COS had established with the poor law: 'What is needed is, not that there should be anything like parallelism between Statutory Relief and Voluntary Assistance, but that exactly opposite relations should subsist. Parallel lines are lines that never meet' (Hancock-Nunn, 1909, p.70). Given that both the state and the COS had failed to organise relief separately, he felt that it was logical to argue that joint machinery and more joint working were needed. In Hampstead he set up a joint committee consisting of five members of the COS, five guardians and five local councillors. After 1903, the board of guardians agreed to refer all cases to the committee, which became the Council of Social Welfare. To Hancock-Nunn this seemed to represent a proper working out of the Goschen Minute of 1869. Goschen had intended that poor relief should be residual. By having all cases come to the Council first, the Hampstead system assured charitable endeavour pride of place.

According to Hancock-Nunn, the vast majority of the cases referred by the guardians were treated by the council. He expressed his hearty dislike of the number of cases that were declared 'ineligible' by the COS. A fellow guardian said that he stood half-way between the school of thought that regarded the administration of the poor law as a deterrent and a means of merely keeping the body and soul of the recipient of relief together, and that of the newer school of guardians, often working men, who wanted to use public funds for more generous relief (Anon., 1942). Hancock-Nunn believed in some form of deterrent, but felt that the human side of the problem of helping the poor should be uppermost. While the focus of the Council was the organisation of relief, it was also concerned with educational, public health (Marks, 1992, has explored these in detail) and cultural issues, cooperating with local authorities in care committee work and in the provision of infant and maternal welfare centres. The Council was prepared to trumpet its approach: 'For the new wine of the spirit of this age we have made new bottles. The names and forms and methods of the COS belong to a generation that is past'.[1] The new organisation boasted a new name 'not clogged with obsolete connotations' and was proud to align itself with local democratically elected bodies, even if Loch regarded it as little more than a jumped-up COS district committee (Loch, 1910).

However, by 1903, Loch was privately advocating cooperation with the new organisations, reminding the Society again of its aim to improve the conditions of the poor and the need actively to combat its image as a negative, inquiry organisation. He urged district secretaries to broaden their outlook and cooperate with other organisations on social questions. He also intimated that voluntary organisations should receive state recognition as part of the organisation of relief, a proposal that seemed to prefigure the recommendations of the 1909 Majority Report to the Royal Commission on the Poor Laws, but Loch did not spell out his ideas in any detail (Loch, 1903). He reiterated his call for more cooperation with the new organisations in 1907,[2] but the COS never accepted Hancock-Nunn's ideas about merging the machinery of charity and the poor law, which threatened the whole way in which they conceptualised the relationship between the statutory and voluntary sectors based on a clear separation of spheres and client groups (Loch, 1916). When Lord Lichfield, whose father had been a founding member of the London COS, tried to form a London-wide Social Welfare Association in 1910, the COS refused to cooperate because it would involve 'municipalisation'. The Society would have had to work wholly in partnership with the LCC on lines similar to the care committees, which would have involved a substantial loss of control.[3]

The guilds of help put much more emphasis on the importance of friendly visiting. Indeed, they seemed to rediscover it. Charity organisation societies in the USA during the Progressive Period always traced the work of visiting back to Octavia Hill and the London Charity

Organisation Society (for example, Richmond, 1899) but, in their anxiety to distance themselves from the COS, the English guilds of help very rarely made any reference to these antecedents, and were in fact more likely to refer to American or German developments (Milledge, 1906). According to the investigation mounted by the Local Government Board in 1911, the general objects of the guilds were to foster a sense of civic responsibility, to provide a friend (or 'helper') for all those in need of help, to discourage indiscriminate almsgiving, to cooperate with other charitable agencies to prevent overlapping, to prevent the poor from sinking into destitution, and to consider the causes of poverty in any particular town. All of these would have found acceptance by one or other of the dominant strands of opinion within the COS and some sympathy is due the members of the COS who complained that the ideas behind the guild movement were not new (Shairp, 1912). In the case of one of the earliest guilds, the Bradford City Guild of Help, only its stress on the importance of uniting citizens of all classes differentiated it from the COS (Milledge, 1906). The guilds adopted the chart devised in 1901 by the influential American social worker, Mary Richmond, to show the 'forces' surrounding the family in the form of kin, neighbours and civic, charitable and public relief agencies (in descending order of importance) on which the helper might draw.[4] But such a list could just as easily have been derived from the publications of the COS. From his study of charity organisation in Manchester, Alan Kidd concluded that the similarities between the new League of Help and the old District Provident Society in respect to their ideas about the importance of visiting and of character was more striking than the League's greater willingness to cooperate with new forms of state social welfare legislation (Kidd, 1984).

Hancock-Nunn suggested that what was happening was the reversal of not so much COS principles as their application. This was not quite accurate in respect of the change in the ideas of many guild members regarding the role of the state, but the main strand of guild criticism of the COS certainly centred on its methods. The guilds accepted the importance of personal social work with the poor, but accused the COS of 'descending' into relief work. In particular they stressed the problem of those who were deemed ineligible for assistance by the COS, something that had attracted criticism from within the Society since the 1880s, and the importance of developing a civic awareness that sought to be inclusive rather than exclusive (Masterman, 1906). The main inspiration for the guilds was the German Elberfield system, by which unpaid workers took on the responsibility for administering relief and doing casework with recipients. The unpaid 'helpers', who were responsible for a maximum of four cases each, were supervised by a 'captain' of their district and captains formed a central board accountable to the city councillors. Octavia Hill had drawn attention to Elberfield as early as 1874 (Hill, 1874) and the *Charity Organisation Reporter* also reported the unsuccessful attempts that were made between 1872 and 1874 to institute an Elberfield system in Macclesfield.[5] Two investigations into the system were made for the Local Government Board, in the early 1870s and the late 1880s. The first of these stressed the extent to which the system involved elaborate surveillance of the poor, which it was felt might prove inconsistent with 'the freedom of English domestic life' (C. 1255, p. 357). (Later on, the guilds were at pains to deny that they entered houses uninvited (Milledge, 1906).) The second, which included a report by Loch, stressed that Elberfield had to be understood as a state scheme of outdoor poor relief operated by unpaid male workers (the role of helper was considered too important to permit women to fill it (Hong, 1989)), who were, in the last instance, forced by law to fulfil their citizenship obligations to volunteer (C. 534). Loch detested both the fact that Elberfield was a system for providing statutory outdoor relief and the municipal and legal control that it exerted over voluntary workers.

However, Julie Sutter, who wrote widely on social issues at the beginning of the twentieth century and sought to publicise the system, admired its sense of civic purpose and approved of the authority given to it by the exercise of municipal control and by male involvement at the visitor level. In her 1901 book on Elberfield she called for the creation of a British National Guild of Help to take the idea forward in Britain (Sutter, 1904). However, she was not happy with the guilds that were established over the next few years: '[they] are an outer shell without the kernel; they are Elberfield without its backbone ... They are pseudo Elberfields. They are Charity Organisation Societies under another name! Like the COS they are devoid of authority – unable to do as they would!' (Sutter, 1907, p. 31). Sutter believed that to be effective the guilds would have to be affiliated to the local authorities and located centrally in the town hall.

The guilds of help took from Elberfield the idea of mobilising all the better off townspeople to help their neighbours in the spirit of personal service. This was something that they might have taken from Bernard Bosanquet, who wrote at length about the importance of the better off fulfilling their citizenship obligations to the poor and of the need for armies of social workers. However, once again the guilds preferred to keep their distance from the COS. For the most part, the guilds did not aspire to become part of a revamped relief system, such as Elberfield represented. Indeed, most wanted firmly to separate relief from friendly visiting, preferring the idea of 'not alms but a friend', the motto of the Boston Association of Charities (Byles, 1908; Grisewood, 1909 (comment in the discussion by S.P. Grundy)). Mary Richmond had stated firmly that those who would be 'friends of the poor, fertile in helpful suggestions, sympathetic and kind' could not also be almoners (Richmond, 1930, p. 41). However, a majority of guilds were quickly sucked into the provision of material aid (Cd 5664), just as the COS had been during its early years. This was particularly ironic, given that guild leaders had begun by criticising the COS for becoming one more relief society (Masterman, 1906). However, Clement Attlee was probably right in the assessment of the guilds' work that he included in his text on social work, published in 1920. While many of the objects and practices of the guilds looked very similar to those of the COS, they exhibited, he felt, a different attitude that appeared both more generous and more democratic (Attlee, 1920, p. 79).

The guilds emphasised the importance of recruiting helpers from the whole population; the Local Government Board investigation reported that 50 per cent of them were working-class (Cd 5664); however from the fragmentary evidence surviving for the Bradford, Halifax, Bolton and Poole Guilds, Laybourne (1993) has concluded that working-class involvement in the movement may have been exaggerated. Some of the leading members of the Bradford City Guild of Help had connections with the new Labour Party: for example, Dorothy Keeling, who became a member of the Guild in 1907 and later secretary of the National Association of the Guilds of Help (Keeling, 1961). Similarly, the guilds insisted that any citizen could be helped. They categorically refused to draw a boundary line between poor law and charity clients, insisting that no-one was 'unhelpable' and stressing the undesirability of the COS practice of abandoning people who were declared ineligible for assistance (Hancock-Nunn, 1909; Milledge, 1906; Masterman, 1906). The COS replied by charging that untrained guild helpers were dealing badly with difficult cases because they lacked firm principles as to the division between the responsibilities of the poor law and charity to guide them. While a minority of delegates attending a 1908 conference on the future of the COS felt that there was much to recommend the 'less cut and dried' methods of the guilds and that the rigorous methods of inquiry demanded by the COS only served to try the patience of the poor and to make the Society unpopular, the majority rejected the position adopted by the guilds on the work of visiting. They saw that it threatened to undermine the division of labour between charity and the poor law which had been derived from the principles of deterrence and, even if many guilds did not want to be subservient in any way to the statutory authorities, that this heralded the beginnings of a more complementary partnership.[6]

There is some evidence that the guild movement was divided as to the extent to which it was prepared either to join forces more formally with the statutory sector in the form of the poor law or to accept government finance (for example, Leach, 1910, argued with Harrison, 1910, on this point at the Annual conference of the North Midland Poor Law Districts in 1910), but unlike the COS it was perfectly prepared to cooperate pragmatically with new state legislation. Like the councils of social welfare, for the most part the guilds welcomed the new liberal welfare reforms. The secretary of the Bradford City Guild of Help felt that the Elberfield system had been easier to organise in Germany because the German state provided pensions and social insurance from an early stage (Milledge, 1906). The Bradford Guild responded positively to the 1906 legislation on school meals and the council's school feeding committee referred the families of poor children to the guild in a spirit of positive cooperation that contrasted with the 'making-the-best-of-a-bad-job' attitude of the London COS (Cahill and Jowitt, 1980). The COS could not accept either this kind of partnership arrangement or even Hancock-Nunn's efforts to devise a relief system that relied on both statutory and voluntary effort, giving the upper hand to charity, because both rode roughshod over the idea of charity as the central guiding social principle. Bernard Bosanquet told the Edinburgh COS in 1907 that those advocating extreme individualism and *laissez-faire* assumed that 'inward grace', good habits and character would be promoted by doing nothing, while collectivists believed that such things could be legislated (Bosanquet, 1907).[7] Only charity understood the need to work with individuals to turn them into socially efficient and fully participatory members of society. Within this framework of belief, charity could not easily be harnessed to statutory provision.

After Loch's call for greater cooperation with the new forms of charity organisation in 1907, the COS set up a committee to investigate the organisation and methods of the Society which reported in 1909. It sought to explore why the COS was unpopular compared to the new organisations and concluded that the chief battle was over social policy. A few witnesses, including Samuel Barnett, suggested that the COS's view of the relationship between charity and the state and its opposition to a larger role for the state was obsolete and repellent to those who wanted to take a more constructive 'civic interest', and asked that the Council of the Society keep quiet about social policy issues.[8] The committee considered whether the Society could abandon its commitment to the methods it believed to be conducive to self maintenance in respect of public policies such as school meals and old age pensions, and pursue them only in its work with individuals. But, while it acknowledged the importance of promoting COS representation on the committees of the new organisations (the Society's usual tactic in face of unwelcome rivals), it concluded by reiterating the old principles of the Society regarding the overwhelming significance of independence and a firm boundary between the work of charity and the poor law in terms of a separation of both client groups and administrative machinery.

While Loch was inclined to make some accommodation with the new organisations,[9] even though he continued to warn against the 'false glamour' of the words 'social welfare' (Loch, 1916), the language of the report produced in 1909 seemed to owe more to the 'hard and dry' strand of opinion within the Society. It played strongly on the importance of economic independence rather than on the principle of reciprocity. A.G. Crowder warned that any relaxation of the Society's views regarding the role of the state in social provision would result in increasing amounts of 'injurious relief given under the guise of coordination and cooperation', while Arthur Clay objected to the establishment of 'statutory official relations' between the voluntary and statutory sectors and defended the maintenance of a clear boundary line between them.[10] Those members of the Society more inclined to a view of statutory/voluntary relations grounded in political economy were also more inclined to resent the new organisations, which appeared to espouse many COS objectives, but which were also critical of its methods and, worse still, gained in popularity as a result.[11] As Bailward commented sadly in 1910, the COS's 'necessary advocacy of economic principles is distasteful to a large section of the charitable public' (Bailward, 1910, p. 74). In a decision that showed how strong the 'hard and dry' strand of opinion within the Society was, the COS rejected the invitation to participate in the first annual conference of the guilds of help, although it did agree to change its name from the Society for Organising Charity and Repressing Mendicity to the Society for the Organisation of Charitable Effort and the Improvement of the Condition of the Poor.

While the COS was agonising about the new personal service societies, the Report of the Royal Commission on the Poor Laws, the first to investigate the poor law since 1832, was set to force the pace of change. Six Commissioners were members of the COS and Helen Bosanquet was largely responsible for drafting the Majority Report (McBriar, 1987). The majority wanted to keep a destitution authority and persisted in locking charity into the framework set by the poor law, holding on to the idea that the statutory and voluntary sectors would deal with different client groups. Hancock-Nunn dissented from this and wrote his Memorandum for the Commission on the work of the Hampstead Council for Social Welfare. However, the majority did favour more joint working between the poor law and charity, arguing that a 'council for voluntary aid' should be set up in each poor law district with more cross representation between it and the poor law authority. The Majority Report also raised the possibility of financial aid for the voluntary sector from the state, and spoke of bringing charities 'into the field of public work and responsibility' with the special task of developing visiting and devising schemes for the mutual registration of cases (Cd 4499, pp. 448, 521–3), despite the close identification of the Bosanquets and Loch with its recommendations. According to Helen Bosanquet's own history of the COS, the Society was unable to campaign on behalf of the Majority Report because it was so split (Bosanquet, 1914). Some were opposed to any change in the poor law. This was true of the hard-line adherents of political economy, such as Mackay (1913) and of Octavia Hill, who had always reserved her criticism for the methods rather than the principles of the Society and who remained firmly convinced as to the merits of a deterrent poor law. As a member of the Commission she formally dissented from the recommendations of the majority. Other members of the Society could not accept the idea that voluntary aid councils might be grant-aided.

The Minority Report, the work of Beatrice Webb, gave a large role to voluntary work in the form of personal service in particular, but placed it firmly under the control of the local authorities (Cd 4499, pp. 1021, 1101). It is tempting to see the Majority Report representing the views of the COS and the minority those of the councils and guilds (Adams, 1976). To some extent the Webbs' campaign to break up the poor laws, conducted in the wake of the publication of the Royal Commission Report, seemed to play on this division. Henry Russell Wakefield, the Dean of Norwich and signatory to the Minority Report, addressed the Bradford City Guild of Help in 1910 and invoked the Elberfield system and the operation of care committees under the auspices of the LCC as examples of the future for voluntary organisations. He ended by advocating the establishment of a guild or council in every local authority to coordinate voluntary work, enlist recruits and make representations to the authority (Dean of Norwich, 1910). Similarly, the Webbs cited the example of Elberfield in terms of the 'organic relationship in which the voluntary helper stands with regard to the Public Authority' and the new possibilities their scheme would offer organisations like the guilds to work with the statutory authorities in providing information and advice – *extensions* to the services offered by the public authorities, rather than separately organised services (Webb and Webb, 1912, p.253). However, some saw the Majority Report as having more in common with the ethos of the guilds and councils (Osborn, 1910). Hancock-Nunn was vehemently opposed to the minority, which he felt ignored the need for coordination between the voluntary and statutory sectors (Hancock-Nunn, n.d.), and, more importantly, proposed an extension of state activity at the expense of the voluntary sector: 'it spells all the bureaucratic paraphernalia of State aid by which, in the long run, the life-blood is sucked out of the nation' (cited in McBriar, 1987, p. 328).

The picture was far from clear-cut because there were many different issues at stake. The Report of the Royal Commission served to focus the issue at the centre of the debates about charity during the Edwardian period: how to draw the boundary between the voluntary and statutory sectors. Some hard-liners within the COS refused to budge from their understandings of the 1869 Goschen Minute. The COS was to be entirely separate from the poor law, but was to cooperate with it in order to make sure that the poor law remained a residual, deterrent authority dealing only with the undeserving/unhelpable. Others, like the Bosanquets and Loch, also defended the idea of a separate destitution authority, but admitted the need for some change in the machinery of the poor law and with it a change in the mechanisms by which it related to charity. Someone like Hancock-Nunn wanted completely to erode the institutional boundaries between the voluntary and statutory sectors, but in such a way that secured primacy of position to charity, while the Webbs also favoured a blurring of the boundary line, but with control passing to the statutory authority and voluntary action becoming supplementary. Both Hancock-Nunn's and the Webbs' options involved abolishing the distinction between charity and poor law clients, something that was anathema to the vast majority of the COS.

Government did not implement the recommendations of the Royal Commission, keeping the poor law as it was and opting instead to remove particular groups of the population – the deserving elderly, children to some extent, and the skilled male worker – from its ambit by making new kinds of provision via pensions, school meals and medical inspections and national insurance. These developments were resisted by the COS, which interpreted them as a dilution of poor law principles, in particular the erosion of any clear idea as to who should be helped by the state and who by charity. The COS was virtually united in its opposition to national insurance in 1911, which according to Loch amounted to unscientific philanthropy on the part of the state.[12] For Bailward, it was another step on the 'slippery slope' to socialism (Bailward, 1920). In contrast, a majority of those involved in the guilds and councils had no problem with the idea of the state becoming the provider of first resort, although many, like Hancock-Nunn, wished to retain a controlling position for charity. The guilds in particular were content to see a division between the sectors based on activities rather than client groups: the state taking primary responsibility for relief and the voluntary sector for social work. British social work's concern to separate itself from the disbursement of money must be traced back to the guilds' desire to shed the COS's involvement in relief alongside the poor law. The majority of guild and council members wished to cooperate with the state on the basis of complementarity, a position that had nothing in common with Loch and Bosanquet's vision of the importance of charity as a social principle.

The ideas of the guilds and councils were reflected in the outside criticism levelled at the COS in the years following the Report of the Royal Commission. Fabian critics accused the Society of being trapped in outdated ideas about the role of the state and in rigid methods. Mrs Townshend's Fabian Tract, published in 1911, described the COS's principles as having 'acquired a kind of sacred character and a strange structure of social theory has been built on [them] that is almost grotesque when compared with everyday experience' (Townshend, 1911, p. 183). The Webbs pressed home their attack, charging that it had proved impossible for the COS either to classify the deserving and the undeserving, or to provide adequately for the former; that the harsh policies of the COS linked firmly to the framework of a deterrent poor law had actually served to promote rather than to restrain sentimental, unscientific charity; and, citing the Elberfield model yet again, that voluntary organisations lacked the power to insist on treatment for those of weak character (Webb and Webb, 1912). The Webbs were quite prepared to mete out harsh treatment to those who might fail to avail themselves of the statutory services they were proposing to offer and to become useful citizens. In their campaign for the Minority Report and the break-up of the poor laws in the years following 1909, the Webbs pushed hard for the abandonment of the 'parallel bars' philosophy of the COS in respect of its relationship with the state, arguing instead for an 'extension ladder' model (ibid., pp. 225–3), in which charity would work in partnership with, but in subordination to, the statutory sector. The Webbs' arguments regarding the proper relationship between charity and the state found a more immediately receptive audience than their ideas for breaking up the poor law.

Criticism from the Fabians was to be expected, but other social activists from different points on the political spectrum joined in, together with the popular press, which was forever taking up particular cases of individual hardship traceable to COS relief practices.[13] Violet Markham who, together with Mrs D.D. Lyttleton, acted as organising secretary to the London-based Personal Service Association, formed in 1908, wrote to the *Spectator* in 1911, arguing that it was difficult to accept the rigid boundary the COS insisted on drawing between state relief for the unhelpable and voluntary relief for the helpable:

> Is it not increasingly difficult to accept the view that the great forces of the state are only to be at the service of the pauper, the lunatic, and the criminal, and that the honest and deserving citizen, if he falls on evil days, should be handed over to what Malthus wrily called 'the uncertain support of private charity'?[14]

Markham invoked the contemporary concern with national efficiency: 'some of us feel that the State cannot for the sake of its own future tolerate a hungry child'; the state had to be not merely repressive and deterrent, but creative. In the correspondence that followed in the *Charity Organisation Review*, she restated her view that the COS stood for 'extreme individualism' and suggested that the Society's insistence on rigid lines of demarcation between its work and that of the state effectively robbed the latter of its best source of advice.[15]

Markham, a Liberal, together with her partner in female anti-suffrage work, Mrs Humphry-Ward, a Conservative, sought to encourage a more positive view of the relationship between charity and the state. Mrs Humphry-Ward eagerly campaigned for state aid for her children's playcentres between 1906 and 1916, when she finally secured a measure of success. Thus the COS was becoming increasingly isolated by insisting on maintaining its firm commitment to separate spheres for voluntary agencies and the state. Markham declared that the guilds of help represented a 'middle course', offering more possibility of growth, and being better adapted to the idea that state action could be creative. But to someone like Bailward, there could be no middle course. State intervention above and beyond relief of the destitute could only do harm (Bailward, 1920, p. 135). In the USA, the older charity organisation societies were prepared to cooperate with social reformers; Mary Richmond saw the relationship between personal service, which she called the 'retail' method of reform, and legislative or 'wholesale' reform as symbiotic (Richmond, 1930, pp. 214–21). But the London COS persisted in seeing them as antithetical because it held to the idea that the practice of true charity alone could build a better social and individual life. This view also imposed a barrier between the COS and the newer forms of charity organisation which was difficult to overcome. A joint conference of the COS, guilds and councils eventually took place in 1914, which led to the setting up of the Joint Committee on Social Service (which in turn became the National Council for Social Service in 1919). The conference had Loch's blessing, but took place against the wishes of hard-liners such as Bailward.

The strength of the COS's desire to preserve its distinctive approach to charity was demonstrated by the decisions it took over its training programme at the beginning of World War I. The work of the School of Sociology, set up by the COS in 1903 and directed by E.J. Urwick, had passed to the London School of Economics in 1912 for financial reasons. As Arthur Clay recorded, many members of the COS were not entirely happy with this solution, feeling that the 'tone and character' of the LSE was at odds with that of the COS.[16] The LSE offered little by way of practical work and, in the view of the COS, the social theory teaching beyond that of Urwick himself left much to be desired. Thus in 1916, the COS approached Bedford College with a view to mounting a course in social work. The Society tried to dictate to the college over the choice of lecturers, wanting Bernard Bosanquet in particular for the course on social ethics. The college resisted this attempt to subvert its academic freedom at the price of having the COS make the agreement for one year only on a renewable basis. As the COS negotiator put it, the Society could not risk the prospect that the character of the college might change and that it might become 'enamoured of lecturers like the Sidney Webbs'.[17]

The war years saw a huge explosion of charitable activity (Prochaska, 1988). Leaders of the guilds and councils were quick to see that the government order setting up Local Representation Committees (LRCs) in each borough of over 20 000 population and in each county district to coordinate relief efforts had major implications for the relationship between charity and the state in the post-war world (D'Aeth, 1915a). D'Aeth (1915a) wanted the LRCs to be permanent, but the COS was, not surprisingly, considerably more cautious. Bernard Bosanquet and the Administrative Committee of the London COS feared for the independence of voluntary organisations,[18] and in this they were joined by Hancock-Nunn (1914), who asked if volunteers were in future to serve the state rather than be participative members of voluntary agencies. In the face of the threat of the 'nationalisation' of charity, the Society turned back to the 1909 recommendations of the Majority Report on the poor laws, floating the possibility of local voluntary aid boards for each town with more than 50 000 people, together with voluntary advisory bodies which would also have statutory representation.[19] However, Bernard Bosanquet continued to defend the complete autonomy of the voluntary sector in the interests of promoting reciprocity, participation and social efficiency. He feared that the new pragmatism regarding cooperation with the state would reduce voluntary action to personal social work in the service of the state: 'I see some new lights inform us from time to time that "casework" alone is to be left to the Charity Organisation Society. The idea would make our founders turn in their graves. Casework which is not handled as an engine of social improvement is not, I should have said, Charity Organisation Society work at all' (Bosanquet, 1917, p. 134).

The COS had seen voluntary personal social work as the only sure way of securing desirable and permanent social change. This perception led it to defend the idea of a firm boundary between the state and voluntary sectors, with a small sphere for the state in the form of a relief system based on deterrence, but, in practice, severe limits were placed on the Society's work by its conception of its relationship to the poor law, which were bound to affect its position when the nature of state provision changed in the early twentieth century. The new forms of charity organisation saw the COS as out of step with new statutory mechanisms for delivering social welfare. The guilds and councils varied in the extent to which they were prepared to see voluntary work tied to the state via joint machinery or financial aid, but they did insist on renegotiating the division of labour between the state and voluntary agencies so that it was task-based rather than client-based. The voluntary agencies would provide friendly visiting and coordinate charitable and state efforts by drawing up mutual registers of those assisted and the like, while the state provided a national minimum level of relief.

In practice, there were many continuities between the COS and the newer forms of charity organisation; many guilds and councils became relief agencies in their turn, but they were determinedly more civic minded and more pragmatic, employing methods that were less 'cut and dried'. However, they offered no coherent rationale for voluntary effort to replace that of Loch and Bosanquet and, while anxious to preserve a large role for charity, were arguably more at risk of having their role defined by the state. During the inter-war years, the partnership between the voluntary and statutory sectors was largely rewritten in accordance with the work of the guilds and councils, but without any broader vision as to the contribution of voluntary action.

## NOTES

1. Hampstead Council of Social Welfare, *Annual Report*, 1908, A/FWA/C/B2/38, FWA Papers, Greater London Record Office.
2. C.S. Loch, 'The Future of Local Charity Organisation', 18 November 1907, A/FWA/A/A1/13/1, f. 178.
3. 'The COS and the Social Welfare Association', 23 May 1910, A/FWA/C/A1/14, f. 148.
4. The chart was reproduced in *Progress*, no. 2 (April 1906), p. 147 and used by the Bradford City Guild of Help to illustrate each case book (Cahill and Jowitt, 1980).
5. 'The Elberfield System', *Charity Organisation Reporter*, 27 March 1872; and 'The Elberfield System', *Charity Organisation Reporter*, 4 March 1874.
6. 'Conference on the Future of the COS', 7 January 1908, A/FWA/C/A1/13/1, f. 290.
7. B. Bosanquet, 'The Social Criterion', paper read to the Edinburgh COS, 1907, Bosanquet Papers, Trunk 1, K6, Newcastle University Library.
8. *Report* of the Special Committee on the Organisation and Methods of the Society, 25 October 1909, A/FWA/A/C/A1/14/1, f. 96.
9. This was also the interpretation of A. Ernest Thomas (1933), secretary of the Middlesbrough Guild of Help.
10. *Report* of the Special Committee on Organisation and Methods.
11. For example, Sir William Chance, 'The assistance of charity, the poor law and the voluntary agencies', 8 July 1912, A/FWA/C/A1/13/1, f. 270.
12. C.S. Loch, letter to *The Times*, presented for consideration by the Administrative Committee, 2 January 1913, A/FWA/C/A3/48/1, f. 114.
13. For example, C.S. Loch, 'The COS and "John Bull"', 23 February 1911, A/FWA/C/A3/46, f. 214.

14. Violet Markham, 'The Problem of poverty', letter to the Spectator, 26/8/11, Markham Papers Pt. II, 28/55, LSE Archives, BLPES.
15. 'Miss Markham on the COS', *Charity Organisation Review*, March 1912.
16. Memorandum for consideration by the Propaganda Sub-Committee of the Administrative Committee of the COS, by A. Clay, 23 May 1916, A/FWA, C/A3/52.
17. Edith Neville (COS) to Miss Melhuish (Bedford College), 24 April 1916, AR/330/1, Bedford College Archives, Royal Holloway College.
18. 'Charities and Public Assistance', 29 July 1915, A/FWA/C/A3/51/1, f. 92.
19. C.F. Adair Hoare, 'War and Peace Charities. The Mobilisation of Voluntary Effort', 8 May 1916, A/FWA/C/A1/15/1, f. 168.

# 4. The inter-war years

In its Annual Report for 1918–19, the Charity Organisation Society reported the passing of the 1918 Child and Maternal Welfare Act, which made the provision of services by local authorities for mothers and children obligatory, commenting gloomily that this was the last of a long series of measures 'aiming at the municipalisation of all forms of public assistance' (COS, 1919, p. 3). The Report acknowledged that the COS had criticised every successive extension of state intervention, but stated that the Society was prepared to be cooperative. This combination of regret for what was perceived as the defeat of the Society's position with a more or less grudging willingness to participate in the new order characterised the public voice of the COS during the inter-war years. The organisation continued fiercely to defend the idea of an autonomous voluntary sector: 'the state-aided voluntary society, to some of us a contradiction in terms, and to some a counsel of despair, is not, we hope, the only alternative to the extinction of voluntaryism' (COS, 1920, p. 4).

Other voluntary agencies were also eager to defend the autonomy of the voluntary sector, but their attitudes towards the state were above all pragmatic. The overwhelming impression of the COS during the inter-war years is of an organisation on the defensive. Furthermore, its opinions no longer automatically commanded attention. The dominant voices of the voluntary sector during the inter-war period were all from outside the COS. In 1920, Clement Attlee suggested that the COS held but a 'minor place' in social service, offering little that was constructive to the post-war world of social provision (Attlee, 1920, p. 67). Attlee paid tribute to the COS's efforts to organise charity, but attributed its failure to a rigid adherence to the boundary between statutory and voluntary action. He accused the COS of individualism and of emphasising the importance of the family as a provider of welfare to the exclusion of the state. This was not an accurate depiction of the COS's own rationale for stressing the importance of the family, which owed more to ideas about the formation of character and citizenship than to economic

individualism. However, Attlee's interpretation was probably not un-
common. He went further still when he pressed home his attack on the
Society, asking why assistance from the state should be deemed inherently stigmatising, something that seemed to make less and less sense
as more groups of people were taken outside the ambit of the poor law,
and charging that the COS emphasised points of character that were the
'most convenient for the wealthier classes. The COS is essentially
designed for the defence of the propertied classes' (ibid., p. 73).

Not many would have supported such an overtly political attack, but
the COS did begin to experience considerable hostility from Labour
councillors during the inter-war years. To some extent this was in the
context of a more generalised suspicion of the voluntary sector. In
1929, the National Council of Social Service (set up in 1919) visited
nearly 60 towns and cities and found a lack of statutory/voluntary
cooperation wherever Labour was in power (Brasnett, 1969). However,
the COS was likely to be singled out for attack. In 1923, the Society
had to abandon its work in Poplar, the home of a Labour-dominated
council and board of guardians, which sought to pay high rates of
outdoor relief (Branson, 1974). In response to the political shifts, it was
no longer rare to find people in the world of charity who sought to fuse
a commitment to Labour party politics with voluntary action, and who
found many aspects of the COS's views, particularly its defence of the
poor law, anachronistic.

Most writing on the voluntary sector in the inter-war period agreed
on a large role for the state and saw this as progressive and desirable. In
an essay on the relationship between the public authorities and voluntary organisations published in 1927, Parker Morris assumed the primacy of the former and suggested that local authorities might assist
voluntary organisations financially, but as the financial responsibility of
the state increased so its control must also increase. To support his
case, he cited the example of nineteenth-century education, initially
funded by the state through voluntary organisations and eventually
provided directly by the state, but whatever model of cooperation was
chosen an historical example could be found. Most writers conceptualised voluntary organisations as pioneers or as providing supplementary
services. Elizabeth Macadam (1934), who came from the settlement
house world and who had become involved in the government initiative
to investigate social work training during World War I, wrapped up the
various forms of interrelationship between statutory and voluntary effort in her idea of a 'new partnership'. She felt that voluntary effort was

most appropriate in schemes that were experimental, in activities that called for flexibility or highly individualised work, or in specialised 'watchdog' activities. There would always be a need for private citizens to 'guard the guardians'.

The main rationales for the voluntary sector that were expressed during the inter-war years were, first, its importance in securing democratic participation and, second, its role in supplementing the services supplied by the state, which it was generally agreed could not afford to do everything. Most writers assumed, like T.S. Simey (1937), that the state should provide 'basic' services. Simey believed that 'the moral authority of the voluntary association has been much weakened in recent years', implying that statutory provision was held in higher esteem (Simey, 1937, p.143). This was a common theme. Constance Braithwaite (1938) felt that as a citizen she had become 'conscious of the superiority of state action over philanthropy in its universality of provision and democratic spirit' and she felt that the state must take responsibility above all for alleviating poverty. The first age of high mass unemployment had clearly removed this task from the purview of charity. This left voluntary action with the task of providing a more flexible 'personal service', supplementary to the state. Casework was generally recognised to be a strength of the voluntary sector. One of the few inter-war contributions clearly to favour voluntary effort over the state was that of J.Q. Henriques (1938). But his adherence to the old deterrent views associated with the poor law and his assertion that state aid should carry stigma failed to find favour with the author of the Foreword to the book, Sir Wyndham Deedes, the Chairman of the London Council of Social Service, who stated firmly that some circumstances were beyond the control of the individual and that state aid was necessary.

Above all, the predominant inter-war view of the voluntary sector was pragmatic. There was no attempt to elucidate a theory of charity in the manner of the COS at the turn of the century. Voluntary action was conceptualised in relation to the state, not on its own account. This also meant that social work, the vehicle chosen by the COS to implement its ideas, was left in a theoretical vacuum. In one of the few philosophical contributions on the role of social work during the period, R.M. MacIver welcomed the increased role of the state in the prevention of poverty in particular, but pointed out that this meant that there were now limits as to what could be hoped for from social work. It could no longer be 'an uplifter' and the sole means of achieving social change, but should rather see its role as providing expert aid to the maladjusted (MacIver, 1931).

This was essentially the kind of casework that Bosanquet had rejected as having nothing to do with the work of charity organisation at the end of World War I. But MacIver had accurately pinpointed the issues that were raised for social work when it no longer occupied a central place in social theory.

## THE CHARITY ORGANISATION SOCIETY AND THE STATE

The Reverend J.C. Pringle, who took over from Loch as the general secretary of the COS in 1914, proved a tenacious defender of COS views about the state. His writings were eccentric, full of long classical references and quotation, and his administrative skills were vastly inferior to those of his predecessor. His acceptance of the extended role of the state in social provision was at best partial. In 1924, he gave a cautious welcome to the idea of extending insurance cover – a reference to the publication of William Beveridge's *Insurance for All and Everything* (1924) – but only because he hoped that, if a scheme of insurance could be found that would tide families over periods of difficulty, it would be possible to return to a poor law that would refuse outdoor relief to the able-bodied (COS, 1924). Pringle kept looking for signs of what he regarded as a return to sanity, that is a return to the principles espoused by the COS in the nineteenth century. He welcomed the more rigorous means-testing that followed in the wake of the Great Crash of 1929 as a step in the right direction and believed that the new Public Assistance Act of 1934 vindicated the COS's belief in the need for a destitution authority, although it would have been more accurate to see the legislation as one more step in the dismantling of the nineteenth-century poor law. He was also much cheered by the fact that the 1934 legislation made provision for casework: 'After a struggle lasting a quarter of a century, in which every single struggle but the last went to the statisticians and wholesalers, their debacle came suddenly' (COS, 1934, p. 9). He was, typically, overstating the case in his desire to clutch at COS straws. Individual casework could never play a large part in modern schemes of social security, but Pringle detested the effort of the twentieth-century state to deal with people in the aggregate rather than on an individual, case-by-case basis.

By the late 1930s, Pringle admitted that the COS had suffered public eclipse. He rewrote COS history as a series of long-drawn-out battles with a state that was determined to dominate the social arena. In this account it was the brave fight put up by the COS that 'resulted in [its] progressive and now long since absolutely complete exclusion from Whitehall and Parliament' (Pringle, 1937, p.215). The *Charity Organisation Review* ceased publication in 1921, to be reborn in 1927 as the *Charity Organisation Quarterly*, which confined itself in the main to articles on the practice of social work. Pringle did sit on the Joint Committee on Social Service, which emerged from World War I with representatives from the guilds of help, the councils of social service, the local representation committees, the COS and central government departments, but he treated it very much as a last line of defence for voluntarism. He did not play a major role in its successor, the National Council of Social Service, to which government looked for cooperation during the inter-war years. The National Council played a major role in work with the unemployed, using central government finance (Harris, 1991).

Nor did the analysis of social problems offered by Pringle during the inter-war years do anything to make the COS more influential. His book on British social services, published in 1933, was an extraordinary polemic against 'mechanistic', large-scale and bureaucratic statutory services. He defended the poor law and deplored the desire to see its role either as filling the gaps left in insurance-based provision, or as a residual provider, both of which he felt entirely misunderstood the principles upon which the poor law was based. He disliked the fact that national insurance was compulsory rather than voluntary, and he believed that a 'character clause' similar to the one that had attached to the provision of old age pensions between 1908 and 1913 (which denied pensions to those with a criminal record or who had been in receipt of poor relief during the past 12 months) should have been part of national insurance legislation. This was to misread the attractions of insurance for both politicians and people. He also played with arguments deploring the self-interest of government employees, which have become more widespread in the last decade, but which in the inter-war years came into conflict with strongly held beliefs about the ethic of public service.

However, the burden of Pringle's argument in his 1933 book and in various articles that he published during the 1920s and 1930s rested on the extent to which the needs of the hard-pressed housewife had been bypassed by the new forms of social service provision. The argument resonated with the COS's traditional concern to bolster the family and its tendency to sympathise more with the working-class mother than with the working-class father. By using the housewife as a mouthpiece for his complaints about the new social legislation, Pringle could also endeavour to look progressive. His sympathetic treatment of the high claims of married women under national health insurance, for example, would have had some appeal for contemporary feminists. From the start of the national health insurance scheme, the sickness rate of married women was high: by 1931–2 they were experiencing 140 per cent more sickness and 60 per cent more disablement than expected. Women active in the labour movement pointed out that women did two jobs and suffered a large amount of illness and disability due to frequent pregnancy, but a 1914 government committee of inquiry concluded that women's claims were excessive, chiefly because of their ignorance of the principles of insurance and because of malingering (Cd 7698, 1914). After continued pressure by the government actuary, the government cut women's benefit rates in 1932. Pringle stressed the 'heroic' toil undertaken by the working-class mother. He agreed that she had failed to develop an 'insurance mind', but said that she could not do so in the absence of a margin for saving. His point was that working-class women were resourceful and responsible, but reforms like national insurance were ill-suited to their needs. While wives were responsible for household budgeting, insurance and dole money went to husbands. In short, wholesale methods of reform ignored the fragile balance of the family economy and did nothing to boost the position of the housewife on whom the health and welfare of the family unit depended. Feminist critics of social insurance also charged that it did nothing to value the work of wives and mothers at home, and made wives wholly dependent on their husbands' contributions and benefits (for example, Fabian Women's Group, 1911). However, as Macadam (1934) pointed out, this did not mean that they favoured the dismantling of the new legislation, as Pringle so clearly did.

In a further volume published in 1937, which purported to be a history of the Metropolitan Visiting and Relief Association, but which in fact provided more by way of commentary on contemporary social arrangements, Pringle made rather more effort to state the COS's willingness to work with the state, and sounded more optimistic as to the possibility of a future for the Society:

> The Family Case-workers who contended so courageously against imposed, flat-rate, mechanically administered old age pensions, have learned

greatly to appreciate that and the similar enactments ... It saves an infinitude of trouble and negotiation to know that this income will be available almost as a matter of course, and that the officers disbursing it have no concern with the personal problems and perplexities of the recipient. ... our members have endeavoured to remove a misunderstanding and to bury a hatchet as tough as some of those in the hills of Odysseus. (Pringle, 1937, p. 63)

While continuing to believe that the COS had lost the war over the principles on which to base social reform, Pringle tried to see how he might carve out a space for the Society. In so doing, he persisted in drawing a boundary line between the COS and the state, which was a very different approach from that of those, like Macadam, who looked for linkages. Pringle was never able to feel comfortable with the idea espoused by the American counterpart of the COS that there was a level below which 'character' could not assert itself and that therefore some national minimum level of state assistance was to be welcomed (Richmond, 1930). Given that, in Pringle's view, 'wholesale' social reform had unfortunately won the day – an invasion by 'barbarous Goths upon the civilized, elegant, philosophical Graeco-Roman world' (Pringle, 1937, p. 209) – the COS needed to regroup around the practice of casework, so that it could offer an individually based service that might mitigate the worse excesses of categorical relief schemes which passed out money with no regard for individual circumstances.

## THE COS AND CASEWORK

It was no longer possible to conceptualise casework as the close associate of the poor law, helping to distinguish the helpable from the unhelpable. Nor was it easy to argue for it as the vehicle for carrying out charity's social purpose because state welfare provision had become so dominant. Instead, Pringle embraced the new psychology to provide a rationale for casework, thereby setting the scene for it to become the *raison d'être* of the organisation rather than a means to a greater end.

Pringle saw in casework a much-needed focus on the individual in the context of his or her family that would redress the balance of standardised state assistance: 'the whole fabric of the public social services is a nightmare to the psychiatric social caseworker, who bears in her eager, devoted hands the torch of civilisation today' (Pringle,

1933, p. 167). Pringle read some of the burgeoning American inter-war literature on casework, particularly that of Mary Richmond and Jessie Taft. Taft was part of the movement in American social work to redefine casework as a 'helping' process using psychodynamic principles. However, there is no evidence that Pringle grasped the new meaning that was beginning to be attached to casework in America. He welcomed the publication of Jung in the Society's Annual Report for 1924–5, but only because he felt that Jung was an excellent propagandist for COS methods (COS, 1925). He liked the use of psychotherapeutic methods in casework because he felt that they sharpened the insistence that the client face up to reality (Pringle, 1937). In other words, Pringle embraced the new psychodynamic dimension to casework because he thought that it added weight to the personal social work that the COS had always believed in. Pringle defined the practice of casework in an early issue of the *Charity Organisation Quarterly* as follows: 'By "casework" perhaps we should explain – the temptation to use professional jargon must always be resisted! – we mean the endeavour to help a neighbour out of his difficulties by bringing to bear upon them every bit of available science' (Pringle, 1927, p. 73). This was suitably vague.

During the inter-war period, developments in the theory and practice of casework took place mainly in the USA. A small and elite corps of psychiatric social workers grew up in Britain during the 1930s, but American ideas about casework only became dominant in Britain after World War II. Then, the COS became a leader in the practice of the new casework, but in the 1930s there is little evidence to suggest that COS social workers changed their practice to any great extent. Changes in the USA were pushed forward by the desire to make social work a distinctive profession and it is significant that, when the COS assimilated the kind of casework that had become common in the USA, it also rapidly turned itself into an organisation staffed by paid workers. However, in Britain during the inter-war years, there was unanimity among commentators on the place of voluntary agencies (which were still staffed mainly by volunteers) that personal social work belonged in the voluntary rather than in the public sector (for example, Simey, 1937). This was in large part a legacy of the strict boundary between the two sectors drawn by the COS in the nineteenth century. In contrast to the USA situation, British personal social work was largely confined to the voluntary sector, something that American commentators had to be careful to explain to their audiences (for example, Bruno, 1937). Social service in the British public sector was called 'social administration' by the 1930s, not 'social work'.

At the American National Conference of Charities and Correction in 1915, Abraham Flexner, noted for his recommendations regarding the reform of the medical profession, asked whether social work was a profession. He came to the conclusion that, while social work was intellectual in character and involved discrimination, analysis and judgement, the social worker was essentially a middleman. His contact with a case had no definite end and no delineated scope. The social worker coordinated and cooperated with others, but the enterprise of social work was 'vague' and often voluntary. Social work could not therefore be considered a profession (Flexner, 1915). Mary Richmond took up the challenge to systematise the body of knowledge that comprised social work in her *Social Diagnosis*, published in 1917. The book elaborated in extraordinary detail the process of investigation, analysis and treatment that comprised the practice of casework. She acknowledged that social questions could be approached via the individual or via the manipulation of larger units; casework was committed to the former and had the possibility of bringing about better adjustments in the social relations between men, women and children. Beginning with the idea of friendly visiting that she attributed to Octavia Hill, she saw the crux of casework as the relationship between worker and client. Soon, she felt, social workers would be recognised by other professionals as people who dealt with the social relations of human beings and would take their place as the natural complement of medical practitioners (Richmond, 1930).

Richmond may be seen as codifying COS best practice shorn of the COS's particular aims and objectives related to its operation alongside the poor law. Her book is a detailed and somewhat relentless exposition of the areas covered by the Occasional Papers published by the COS on casework before World War I. Una Cormack (1945, p. 104), writing from the perspective of a psychodynamic caseworker, felt a certain distaste for the rigour of Richmond's exposition: 'Throughout the whole book the interviewer, as it were, shoots a sitting duck, plucks him, trusses him, bastes him, and dishes him up finally settled "in his right relation to society".' A specimen casepaper published by the COS shows that good practice in the Society had the elements demanded by Richmond's method (COS, n.d.). However, as A.L. Hodson's testimony showed, many COS workers were entirely unclear as to how to *do* casework. In 1929, a committee set up by the Milford Conference in the USA produced a report defining social casework (Milford Conference, 1929). It concluded that social casework was a definite entity and social work a unified profession, but that the practice of casework was more precise than its philosophy. The opposite conclusion would have been more appropriate in the case of the COS .

American casework went on to seek theoretical legitimacy for its work in the new psychology and psychoanalysis. Virginia Robinson described the way in which analytic therapy was seized upon to provide knowledge of family relationships in terms of the emphasis it put on needs rather than character. This meant that casework proceeded to search for the individual's needs as a first step in diagnosis, and to focus then, not on material provision, but on the symbols by which needs had expressed themselves (Robinson, 1930). Case papers informed by psychoanalytic principles were very different from the older, more sociological, documents. There was increasing detail on behaviour, attitudes and relationships between family members, and less on social and economic circumstances. To the extent that this kind of approach tended to put more distance between social work and money, it might be expected to have been popular with the alternative forms of charity organisation that grew up in Britain in the early part of the century. However, there is little evidence that psychodynamics penetrated British social work before the 1950s (Yelloly, 1980). There was only one British course in psychiatric social work, set up at the London School of Economics (LSE) in 1929.

The only area of practice in which various ideas from dynamic psychology and psychoanalysis came to exercise a strong influence in Britain during the 1930s was child guidance. The new psychology posed a challenge to old ideas about habit and character by opening 'the possibility that the will, the emotions and the passions were not simply fuel driving behaviour which was then to be controlled by conditioning but that they were part and parcel of an individual psychology' (Urwin and Sharland, 1992, p. 183). However, developments in British child guidance were driven as much by psychiatric medicine and a preoccupation with the need to 'discover' hereditarian defects as by psychodynamics (Thom, 1992). Sybil Clement Brown, who was among the handful of social workers trained by the Commonwealth Fund in New York in the new methods of child guidance, compared a sample of social work case records for 1924 and 1934 and suggested that there had been a substantial shift away from a preoccupation with issues like honesty and sobriety, to personality and family relationships

(Brown, 1939). As Rose (1985) has stressed, the new psychosocial strategy that was applied to maladjusted and delinquent children during the inter-war period made it possible for the problem to be located not in circumstances but in feelings about circumstances, which in turn meant that the relationship of the social worker to the mother could become therapeutic. Nevertheless, as late as the mid-1940s, Brown showed no sign of giving psychology or psychoanalysis pride of place in her definition of social work (Brown, 1945).

In the case of COS practice, there was a tendency for voluntary casework to operate in areas not covered by the state. At a 1936 meeting about the future of the Society, one social worker said that she felt that her own district committee 'had unconsciously drifted into being the suppliers of spare parts not provided for by (a) Statutory Bodies and (b) other voluntary agencies'.[1] Benjamin Astbury, a committed caseworker, who followed Pringle as general secretary of the COS in 1938, raised a number of points about casework in a paper he wrote in 1931. He wondered whether in respect of most of his clients he was carrying out casework or merely making it possible for them to obtain some temporary form of monetary assistance: 'we can bandage the wound and supply crutches to a man, but only the man himself can walk' (Astbury, 1931, p. 3). In a paper he gave to the Second International Conference on Social Work in 1938, he reported that 80 per cent of the applications to the COS consisted of people wanting dentures, clothing or convalescence. He went on to say that in almost all cases an 'underlying' problem was found, for example faulty domestic management or debt, but the vast majority of COS offices reported that they had no time to deal with these (Astbury, 1938). Astbury was groping towards the new practice of casework, but it would seem that the COS was still experiencing difficulty disentangling the work of friendly visiting from relief, let alone trying to tackle the problems of 'bad habits', or, as they had become for Astbury, the 'underlying problems' impeding 'self-adjustment'. Astbury's description of the ideal casework practice continued to emphasise the importance of restoring the individual to self-maintenance, but he was beginning to think of this as a professional task involving an understanding of personality and relationships and as a process of adjusting the balance between the individual and his environment.

Both Pringle and Astbury, albeit in very different ways, sought to make casework the *raison d'être* of the COS. E.J. Urwick, who by the inter-war years was a professor in the Department of Social Service at the University of Toronto, viewed this development with horror. Urwick's passionate attack on social work as casework amounted to a defence of Loch and Bosanquet's social philosophy and in particular of their emphasis on the importance of the principle of reciprocity. His attack undoubtedly gained in force from his being located in North America: Urwick had seen the future of social work and did not like it. He had no quarrel with the extension of state intervention – indeed, he had been one of the very few members of the COS not to have raised objection to the state provision of school meals, suggesting that if the state helped in this way it would merely enable the family to get on with the all-important task of socialising its members (Urwick, 1912, p. 197). His concern was focused entirely on the meaning of social work, which he insisted on locating in the discourse on citizenship. Citizens, he argued, were born debtors, not creditors, and citizenship had no meaning unless it was earned by personal service to others. He deplored the idea that the science of psychology could supply a sufficient rationale for social work; it amounted to 'the belittling – the appalling belittling – of all that we mean by social work and by social life and its difficulties' (Urwick, 1930, p. 15).

The problem to be solved was not of minds waiting for satisfactory adjustment to their environment, but of a 'soul struggling with the infinite complexity of its own nature and its own life'. Just as Loch and Bosanquet rejected any simple reliance on the principles of political economy, so Urwick in his turn urged a healthy suspicion of what psychology could offer. For Urwick, social work could never be just a simple matter of diagnosis and treatment: to make it such was to reduce it to 'the ancillary of specialised medical treatment'. Properly performed, social work could not encompass 'treatment' *per se*, because treatment inferred passivity, which denied the principle of reciprocity. Urwick was also perceptive in linking the eclipse of older COS ideas to a growing impatience with the injunction to duty and service which late Victorians had found so powerful. The philosophy of Bertrand Russell (1916) and George Moore (1968) explicitly rejected the concept of duty, and some of those who in the early twentieth century followed the new thinking in their pursuit of creative impulse and desire, rather than the cultivation of 'best selves', also turned to the new psychology in the inter-war years.

Urwick's real protest was against social work becoming a set of skills divorced from larger social principles, and an end in itself rather than a means to the greater end represented by the practice of true charity. In 1930, the picture he painted of contemporary social work held true only for North America, but by the 1950s it would hold good for Britain and especially for the COS. Urwick was prescient in seeing that the new social work, defined as casework and based on psychodynamic principles, would have difficulty in supporting a social work profession. However, the problems of the COS in the inter-war years were somewhat different. No longer in the forefront of opinion making on social issues, the Society appeared to be in decline. The number of district committees declined from 40 to 21 and, more fundamental, the Society appeared defensive as to its purpose and practice. Under Pringle it continued to show reluctance in accepting the increased role of the state in social provision and only latched onto the new literature on casework in order to reaffirm its traditional practice. It was ironic that in terms of its actual work the Society found itself preoccupied with meeting the material needs that were still not provided for by the state. This would change immediately after World War II, when the demand for dentures, for example, under the National Health Service reached legendary proportions. With Astbury there were signs that the Society was reaching an accommodation with the role of the state, as well as a better understanding of the changes in literature on casework; Astbury's address to the 1938 International Conference on Social Work showed a considerably more pragmatic approach to state provision than did Pringle's (Astbury, 1938; Pringle, 1938). But the COS was adjusting to developments that it had played no part in forging.

## NOTE

1. Miss Nora Hill, 'The COS at the Cross-Roads', 24 February 1936, A/FW/C/A1/18/ 1, f. 69, FWA Papers, Greater London Record Office.

# PART II
# The FWA

# 5. Specialising in casework, 1940s to 1960s

The COS changed its name to the Family Welfare Association in 1946. Beveridge felt the change had two implications: 'It meant not only passing over from charity in the sense of giving money, to the giving of constructive help and guidance apart from money. It meant also passing from being an agency in general to being one with special interests' (Beveridge, 1948, p. 143).

Beveridge was a stout defender of voluntary action. He was invited to address the COS's annual general meeting in 1943, the year after the publication of his report on social insurance, which laid out a scheme for the social protection of all citizens based on the assumption that there would also be a National Health Service, family allowances and full employment. But, as he sought to reassure the members of the COS, since what the state provided had to be the same for all citizens, there would always remain scope to provide individual care for those who needed something more or different. Beveridge intended state provision as a national minimum, which left plenty of room for social provision above that minimum. In particular, he believed that many things could not be accomplished simply by the redistribution of resources. Money was not everything and there was a need for services 'which often cannot be bought with money, but may be rendered from sense of duty' (ibid., p. 320). Beveridge had a clear picture of voluntary organisations as autonomous and driven by social conscience and a strong belief in the importance of this kind of distinctive private enterprise: 'a society which gives itself up to the dominance of the business motive is a bad society' (ibid., p. 322).

Nevertheless, this was fundamentally different from the Charity Organisation Society's early conception of the relationship between charity and the state, which aimed to make charity the central organising social principle. Beveridge used the word 'supplementary' in his writing on voluntary action to describe the work of voluntary organisations in relation to the state, something that Loch and Bosanquet would have deplored. After World War II, the FWA was increasingly obliged to define itself in relation to statutory services. In many ways it may be considered successfully to have marked out a distinctive territory of service in the form of family casework, in which it came to occupy a dominant position of leadership during the 1960s. However, the FWA was far from a unified organisation. The work relating to the administration of trusts on the one hand and personal social work on the other had dovetailed in the old COS, where, notwithstanding the commitment to friendly visiting, so much personal social work had consisted of making decisions about who warranted material help from charity rather than the poor law. But as social work in the form of casework became progressively divorced from money, the parts of the FWA tended to become separate empires. In addition, the Association faced considerable external turbulence as social work became increasingly professionalised and a part of the statutory sector, a process accelerated first by Eileen Younghusband's report on local authority social workers, published in 1959, and later by the 1968 Seebohm Report, which resulted in the setting up of unified social services departments. From being the kind of service that Beveridge and other post-war commentators had seen as being quintessentially voluntary, casework became something that it was hoped to make accessible to all families. In a sense this could be considered a victory for the FWA, although there was always also a strong current of external criticism of social work defined as casework. The name of the FWA was synonymous with good casework practice by the 1960s, but it was left with the problem of differentiating its work from that of the local authority and of persuading local authorities that there was reason to fund what was an increasingly expensive, intensive casework service.

## REDEFINING THE TERRITORY OF THE FWA IN THE 1940s

The COS sponsored a conference at the Institute of Sociology in Oxford in 1941 to discuss social reconstruction. Participants agreed that they were 'looking for a new thing' in social service.[1] The sense of being in transition was strong in the COS of the 1940s, in terms of the movement from unpaid to paid social work, and towards a much greater role for the state. Some members of the COS felt that the organisation should offer a more advice-oriented service, building on the Citizens' Advice Bureaux (set up at the beginning of the World War II to help the ordinary citizen negotiate the mass of wartime legislation) that the organisation controlled in London. Others wanted a more psychologically oriented model of social work. But the senior district secretaries and the general secretary, Benjamin Astbury, tended to the view that, if material aid was to become primarily the province of the state, it was logical for the COS to offer a complementary casework service, something the COS had argued for throughout the inter-war years, although some district secretaries expressed anxiety that such an individualist focus made the COS look reactionary.[2] In fact, the COS came to a firm decision early in the 1940s to support the extension of state welfare, unlike its at best ambivalent position of the 1920s and 1930s. In 1942, a special committee on family allowances, which included outside representatives, recommended a weekly payment of eight shillings (higher than was legislated in 1945, although slightly lower than Beveridge wanted) payable to the mother.[3] The problem was more how to take the COS's own work forward.

The COS solicited outside opinions on this issue, turning first to Eileen Younghusband, who had joined an LCC care committee in Stepney in the 1920s, taken the LSE social science course and worked for the Stepney FWA committee in her vacations, managed a Citizens' Advice Bureau and who, in 1942, was the chairman of the National Council of Girls' Clubs (Jones, 1984). She based her comments on the assumption that the COS was primarily an organisation devoted to personal social work and expressed the view that it was efficient but out-of-date, and had done little to take forward family casework as a profession.[4] Cherry Morris, an almoner, whose book on casework was first published in 1949 and represented the first sustained British contribution on the subject, also criticised the COS, for spending too much time on 'ponderous investigation for the performance of small services',[5] in a letter she addressed to *Social Work* (a quarterly review of family casework, which the FWA continued to publish from 1939 to 1965). All commentators, internal and external, also urged the organisation to change its name. In response, Astbury (1943) agreed that the COS should take the initiative in social casework. The possibility of making CAB advice work the centre of COS endeavour was never seriously considered. The CAB service was new and its administration was shared with the London Council of Social Service. The traditions of the COS were firmly rooted in Victorian and Edwardian ideas of personal social service, which, after all, had been referred to as 'casework' since the end of the nineteenth century.

In many ways the COS proceeded to justify its role as a provider of a family casework service on the lines set out by MacIver in 1931.[6] Accepting the post-war Labour government's commitment to social welfare legislation as a *fait accompli*, when the members of the COS asked themselves what an organisation such as theirs could contribute, the answer often seemed to be 'to help those people who are unable to take advantage of the help provided by the State'.[7] This line of argument was signalled by the 1941 Oxford Conference, which felt that too much attention was being paid in the debate over social reconstruction to the importance of full employment and too little to helping misfits. Such an argument provided the space for work with individuals in the welfare state. Cherry Morris's (1954) book emphasised that casework, by taking an individual approach to need, represented a means of reconciling the rival claims of welfare and freedom.

By the end of World War II the argument for the casework pioneered by the voluntary sector, which was put strongly by the COS to Beveridge's Social Insurance Committee, was widely accepted.[8] In her second report on social work for the Carnegie UK Trust, Eileen Younghusband referred to the fact that there was (in 1951) a better understanding of the kind of 'personal, long-term' individual social work that was 'best performed by voluntary societies' (Younghusband, 1951, para. 2). Similarly, the 1952 Nathan Committee Report on charities referred to 'two streams, appropriate individual care for the individual casualty, together with state action to control the causes of distress' (Cmd 8710, para 47). This kind of analysis resulted in the public acceptance of the kind of boundary between the voluntary and the statutory sector, based on a division of tasks, that the guilds of help had argued for and which had begun to become apparent in the inter-war years. However, it was not to last for long, as the professionalisation of social work sought to broaden the constituency for casework and also carried it into the statutory sector.

## REDEFINING CASEWORK

At the end of the 1940s, the FWA underwent radical reorganisation, reducing the number of district committees from 21 to nine 'areas' in 1948, and again to seven in 1954. While the commitment to casework was clear, its meaning remained contested. During the inter-war years, Pringle had welcomed the new American literature on casework without substantially changing the COS's understanding of the term. By the beginning of the 1950s, it was recognised that casework meant something different from the personal service of the early part of the twentieth century, although the shift was by no means easy or even complete. Not until the American model of psychologically dominated casework fully penetrated British casework during the rest of the decade did the FWA achieve a fluent definition of the new casework and a renewed commitment to its practice.

British social work was hardly swept away overnight by the psychological deluge (Yelloly, 1980). As Younghusband observed in her 1951 report, most social workers were preoccupied with their inter- and intra-professional relationships and the equipment necessary to improve training and professional standards. With regard to the latter, social workers turned increasingly to psychodynamic work, but this was by no means universally accepted and proved difficult to achieve. In local government social work, for example, medical officers of health were not receptive to the practice of casework in the public health departments and on the whole tended to favour the approach of the health visitor (Collis, 1958). Lay members of FWA district committees were also inclined to express reservations.

In the early 1940s, the FWA moved more firmly away from a casework practice that was designed both to educate and to categorise for purposes of relief, and towards one built on psychodynamic principles that were universally applicable (albeit that the FWA continued to deal with clients who were poor). The FWA began to emphasise the importance of discovering and treating the underlying causes of particular kinds of behaviour,[9] and by the end of the decade more stress was being put on the aim of 'adjusting' the individual to his environment. A.T.M. Wilson (1947), of the Tavistock Institute, defined casework as a process that developed personality through consciously effected adjustments between the inner and outer worlds. He suggested that the fundamental procedures of casework were the same, no matter the setting or client group, and consisted of diagnosis and the establishment of a relationship through which treatment would take place. Una Cormack presented a similar definition to the FWA's Aims and Policy Committee in 1949,[10] which was elaborated during the early 1950s, setting out clearly the aim – 'adjustment' – and the method – 'relationship'. The latter was said to be grounded in the worker's understanding of human behaviour and knowledge of social resources and served to build up the inner capacity of the client by releasing the feelings and anxieties that hindered adjustment.[11] However, some members of the FWA continued to question this idea of casework and to stress the importance of common sense, experience, vocation and character as the essentials for good practice.[12]

The FWA was not alone in stumbling over the new definition of casework. In a 1950 inaugural lecture on social work, Professor Roger Wilson noted that many voluntary organisations were finding it difficult to make the transition from casework tied to the giving of relief to casework oriented towards social relationships (Wilson, 1950). In 1953, the Ministry of Health was still defining a social worker as someone who 'visits people in their homes as an advisor and in connection with statutory duties'.[13] Nor was there any evidence that the general public had any idea as to what casework meant. As Eileen Younghusband pointed out, in an FWA survey of casework in two rural areas, practically no-one, official or other, knew the meaning of casework services (Foreword to Smith and Bate, 1951). Noel Timms found that nothing much had changed ten years later, when all but 2 per cent of his 144 interviewees had heard of the probation officer, but only 7 per cent had heard of the social caseworker (Timms, 1962).

However, leaders in the social work field recognised that casework had become something very different from personal service by the early 1950s. Younghusband's first (1947) report on social work for the Carnegie UK Trust stressed the importance of casework and argued that some experience of family casework was a necessary prerequisite for all social work students before they started to specialise, but it put little emphasis on the psychological component of social work training and made no reference to the casework relationship. However, her second (1951) report called for social work training to provide a better understanding of human motivation and experience because social work was centred on human relationships. Younghusband cited the American literature in arguing for the importance of self-awareness and for the connection between accepting others and facing oneself, although she stopped well short of suggesting that social work training be dominated by psychology and psychoanalytical methods. Nevertheless, as her contribution to Cherry Morris's volume on casework showed, she had become aware that psychology had shattered the old frameworks within which casework had been practised.

Two special projects undertaken by the FWA in the early 1950s did much to refine the concept of casework within the Association. One provided marriage guidance through what came to be called the Family

Discussion Bureaux and the second focused on 'problem families'. Both arose out of the concerns of the immediate post-war period. Most commentators emphasised the need to 'rebuild' the family after the war (for example, Marchant, 1946). Concern about the dislocation caused by evacuation and intensive bombing and the consequent disruption to family life, together with anxiety about the rise in the illegitimacy and divorce rates and the falling birth rate, was widely expressed. It was feared that family life had disintegrated during the war and, in the face of this, doctors and religious leaders in particular felt the need to return to first principles, stressing the fundamental importance of the family unit and its profound 'biological significance' (for example, Spence, 1946). In the case of marriage, members of the Marriage Guidance Committee (MGC) highlighted the problems of extramarital conceptions and divorce in a series of polemical publications (see, especially, Mace, 1945) that were discussed in the course of a House of Lords debate on sexual morality and the family in May 1946. The MGC also began to stress the cost of the increase in marriage breakdown to the Exchequer in terms of legal aid (freely available after 1946) and welfare benefits (Mace, 1948). The Committee argued that in a rational, planned post-war society the family also needed help. In 1946, a National Marriage Guidance Council (NMGC) was formed and mounted a campaign for government funding, which was successful in 1949. The CAB also urged the development of a service 'to help in rebuilding the large number of marriages which were on the verge of complete breakdown and, by educative methods, to prevent such conditions arising' (FWA, 1946). During 1945–6, the FWA paid the MGC to train 30 workers for six CAB centres. But in 1947, the FWA decided to continue its marital work on somewhat different lines, believing that it put too much strain on CAB workers.

With the aid of a Goldsmith's Company grant it started two new centres in London and set up a Marriage Welfare Sub-Committee, which included two staff members from the Tavistock Institute, Professor A.T.M. Wilson and Isobel Menzies, a lay analyst, and the two founders of the Peckham Health Centre (Scott Williamson and Innes Pearse), which was set up in 1926 to investigate the nature of health and the conditions necessary for its maintenance. The Centre operated on the premise that the married couple constituted the basic biological unit of society and concentrated its efforts towards promoting the orderly growth and development of family life (Pearse and Crocker, 1943; Lewis and Brookes, 1983). The Sub-Committee agreed that 'marriage welfare work was an integral part of family case work, and must include in its approach a study of inter-personal relationships in the family as a whole, and of the family as a unit in a larger group in the community'.[14] This part of the new basis for the FWA's marriage welfare work was clearly influenced by the Tavistock Institute, which was to play a major role in the development of the project. The Sub-Committee also agreed that it would be 'most helpful to approach the problem from the angle of the healthy marriage to try to find out at what stage tensions and difficulties arose rather than to try to cure marriages already nearly at breaking point'. This reflected the Peckham Health Centre's emphasis on the importance of studying 'normal' families. In its first formal report, the Sub-Committee echoed the findings of the Peckham Health Centre in the stress it placed on the isolation of families, the lack of 'real' family life and the general 'malaise' in the communities served by the FWA's centres.[15]

The shift in the nature of the FWA's work led to competition rather than cooperation between the FWA and the NMGC during 1948 as they vied for advantage in their representations to government for financial support. At bottom the argument revolved around the emerging ideas as to the proper basis for marital work. In a lengthy memorandum prepared at the request of the Home Office in June 1948, A.T.M. Wilson stressed the importance of the revolution in casework practice that was occurring.[16] Social work, he argued, was becoming increasingly aware of the need to move away from the middle-class idea of personal services to families in economic distress and towards the psycho-analytically inspired concern with relationships within the family. He argued that voluntary casework must 'dissociate itself from overt attempts to deal with material need' if it were to tackle new problems and appeal to more than working-class people. This was one of the first explicit appeals for family casework to shift its ground to the psychodynamic. Wilson held up the idea of new family casework methods to the FWA as an approach designed to bridge past aims to achieve individual self-maintenance in a material sense and the new preoccupations with self-support on the basis of normative adjustment.

Wilson also contended that marital problems were complex and not susceptible to amateur intervention. He warned that a commonsense approach (often referred to as desirable by the proponents of marriage guidance) was particularly inappropriate and even dangerous to the client. Lay counselling in marriage guidance could be but an 'unfortunate stop gap' in Wilson's view. The way forward was to be found in experiments like the Family Discussion Bureaux where professional caseworkers would receive a more thorough psychodynamically informed training (by Wilson). The Home Office, if not Parliament, which remained attached to the idea of volunteers lending a sympathetic ear to couples in marital difficulties, tended to agree with Wilson's views. A Departmental Minute of December 1949 recorded that the FWA seemed to be more aware of the complexity of the problem and to propose a more 'scientific and flexible' approach.[17] The FWA and the NMGC, together with the Catholic Marriage Advisory Council, all received grants from the Home Office in 1949.

By 1954, the FWA considered that the Family Discussion Bureau (FDB – the two centres were merged in 1951) had emerged as a specialised and deliberately non-medical agency, although it admitted that it had proved difficult to draw the line between the work of the caseworkers and that of the Tavistock's psychiatric clinic. The social workers were said to have gained an understanding of interpersonal relations that helped them in the work of diagnosis and treatment.[18] The focus of their work was not on working with both partners to try and effect reconciliation, but rather on the individual and trying to understand what she or he was doing in the marriage, what was being unconsciously expressed for her or him by the other, and which of her or his own internal conflicts she or he was unconsciously trying to solve in what was going on (Bannister *et al.*, 1955; Pincus, 1962). The FDB developed the use of the 'therapeutic pair' with client couples and placed a growing emphasis on the way in which the relationship between the therapists could reflect problems within the couple relationship, highlighting the importance of case conferences for these elements to be explored by the whole group and not just the therapists. At the end of its experimental phase, in 1956, the FWA decided to hand the FDB over to the Tavistock Institute, for reasons that remain obscure, but the project had made a decisive contribution in terms of demonstrating the extent to which social workers could practise psychodynamically informed casework; the medical director of the Tavistock Clinic believed that caseworkers could be taught to use psychotherapy (Sutherland, 1957).

A second experimental project with problem families during the first half of the 1950s also helped to redefine casework. The government committee appointed to inquire into 'mental deficiency' in 1924 emphasised that the problem was primarily a question of heredity and was the first to raise the possibility of the existence of a 'social problem

group' (Board of Education and Board of Control, 1927). In the wake
of this, strenuous efforts were made to establish the precise size and
characteristics of the social problem group, with a view to segregating
its members and possibly sterilising them, if public opinion could be so
persuaded (a Departmental Committee of the Ministry of Health recommended voluntary sterilisation in 1934 (Cmd 4495)). A social survey of Merseyside concluded in 1934 that 'from the main discussion ...
a sub-normal type of family has emerged as the "villain of the piece",
parading under one or more disguises, sometimes under the cloak of
unemployment, sometimes dependent on public assistance, sometimes
living in overcrowded conditions, but all alike above the average in
fertility' (Jones, 1934, p. 543). In 1937, C.P. Blacker, the secretary of
the Eugenics Society, listed the characteristics of the social problem
group as 'insanity, epilepsy, occupational instability, inebriety and
social dependency...' (Blacker, 1937, p. 4). This analysis and the
solution, which involved some form of segregation to stop the trans-
mission of these undesirable characteristics, was in line with the idea
that when family failed – the measure being primarily one of economic
dependence – then nothing further could be done.

During the 1940s, the social problem group became the 'social problem family'. Blacker explained this transition by referring to the experience of wartime evacuation and a shift from an 'impersonal, sociological to a personal and human approach' (Blacker, 1952, p. 12). This
was very much an *ex post facto* rationalisation. In fact, the studies
published in the mid-1940s, chiefly by the medical officers of health
employed in local authority public health departments, continued firmly
to emphasise mental deficiency as the major cause of family failure and
the crude use of animal imagery in many of the descriptions of the
characteristics of problem families indicated that they were believed
incapable of living a 'normal' family life (Savage, 1946; Brockington,
1949; Wofinden, 1950). The Women's Group on Public Welfare, which
had produced an influential report on the condition of child evacuees in
1943 under the title *Our Towns*, went on to publish a second report on
*The Neglected Child and His Family* in 1948, which concluded: 'In
looking at these problem families there emerges one dominating feature – the capacity of the mother' (p. 22). The Group criticised what
they viewed as the confusion of intellectual with mental defect in the
medical studies, pointing out that problem mothers were certainly
appallingly ignorant, but that most appeared to genuinely love their
children, who, while improperly cared for, seemed also to love their

parents. These were not affectionless families, as the efforts of mothers to reclaim their evacuated children proved, and where there was affection it was felt that it should prove possible to educate mothers to a more mature understanding of their duties. This view was accepted by the Pacifist Service Units (the forerunner of the Family Service Units) which sought to 'rehabilitate' problem families. The PSU employed the concept of casework to describe their work, by which they meant something more than visiting, but did not use psychodynamic methods. Tom Stephens (1946, p.45) described the family casework of the PSU as 'a matter of helping one's neighbours out of difficulties, enabling them to live fuller and more satisfying lives, and guiding them towards the realisation of the best in their lives and in themselves'. In a sense, PSU workers took Octavia Hill's ideas about changing habits seriously, working alongside a family, scrubbing floors if necessary, until new habits were learned. Stephens defended the work of the PSU by saying that, while it might look as though PSU workers were relieving parents of their responsibilities by painting rooms or even paying the rent in some cases, they were in fact exerting pressure on the parents, because the worker's own willingness to do the job brought home the responsibility to the parents.

The FWA's interest in problem families stemmed initially from the fact that some districts were reporting that as many as 75 per cent of their caseloads fell into this category.[19] The definition of such families varied between districts, but was agreed by the Association in 1947 to be: 'Families who because of physical or mental incapacity or the failure to recognise moral obligation, are unable to live in accordance with normal standards or to benefit from the Services provided by the Community for their health and well-being without skilled personal service given intensively over a long period'.[20] Once the problem of 'problem families' was defined in terms of incapacity rather than dependence, then they became part of the group who needed help to take advantage of the new state services, whom the FWA had identified as being its special responsibility. This, as Richard Titmuss recognised, represented an important addition to the administrator's view of social service provision (Foreword to Philp and Timms, 1957). In his *The Neglected Child and the Social Services*, David Donnison (1954) recommended the setting up of an extended specialised family casework service, either through the local authorities or through voluntary organisations.

The FWA emphasised, not so much 'the aetiology' of problem families, but treatment using 'relationship therapy'.[21] In fact, the project mixed old and new ideas about casework. Workers were explicitly encouraged to pursue the 'not-alms-but-a-friend' approach of earlier generations of visitors, with the aim of restoring the client to 'self-reliance' and active participation in society. But workers also used the idea that it was necessary to understand the emotional needs behind particular behaviour.[22] By 1954, it was being suggested that problem families should be classified according to the different use they made of the casework relationship (Irvine, 1954).

FWA practice more generally in the 1950s was nevertheless mixed. There were only 26 caseworkers in the seven areas, which meant that many teetered on the edge of viability, but the Association was forever having to steer a difficult course between the Scylla of staffing and the Charybdis of finance. In addition, a considerable amount of the FWA's work still related to material needs, as Rosalind Chambers pointed out in her appendix to Barbara Wootton's influential attack on the new casework, published in 1959.

The reorganisation of the Association at the beginning of the 1950s resulted in two experimental areas regarding methods. In one of these, the area secretary had taken a course in casework at the Tavistock Institute and workers in these areas were involved in teaching students from the LSE's new generic social work course, funded by the Carnegie UK Trust and directed by Eileen Younghusband (Hartshorn, 1982). These two areas practised more intensive social work and workers had lower caseloads than elsewhere, something that was initially opposed by one of the area committees in 1951 (Donnison and Chapman, 1967). These areas also sought to provide professional supervision for case-workers and to instigate case conferences run by paid caseworkers to take the place of the old voluntary committee member meetings which took decisions on clients in the days of the COS. In other areas the power of lay committees remained intact at the end of the decade. Some lay committee members expressed considerable unease about the new casework and about any move towards the adoption of the 'psychological aspects' of the methods associated with the Tavistock Institute,[23] despite the recognition by the Aims and Policy Committee in 1953 as to the need for professionalisation if the agency was to maintain its position in the field.[24] Muriel Cunliffe, a Canadian social worker, who made two visits to Britain during the 1950s to give seminars on casework supervision and who agreed to review the FWA at the end of the decade, found it necessary to point out that supervision was not a crutch for poor workers but a means of transforming the way in which the agency treated its clients (Cunliffe, 1958). In fact, even the two experimental areas found it difficult to secure supervision for staff. A psychiatric social worker was appointed in 1954, but she devoted most of her attention to the non-experimental areas. Various grants secured temporary supervision from American caseworkers in the mid-1950s, although there was some confusion as to whether these women were intended to train FWA staff to supervise, or provide supervision themselves. In 1956, the Association turned to the FDB for help, but the Bureau's help was limited to marital cases. A casework consultant was not appointed until 1963.

The movement of the FWA towards the practice of the new casework meant that clients had to be carefully selected. As part of its radical reorganisation at the beginning of the decade, the FWA arranged for the regional psychiatrists attached to the regional hospital boards of the NHS to visit its offices on a regular basis to advise on selection and other elements of practice. Ironically, these people tended to reject many FWA clients as 'unhelpable', something that annoyed some caseworkers (Keenleyside, 1958) as much as similar practices, albeit for different reasons, had caused dissension in the late nineteenth century. Eileen Younghusband (1951, para. 204) also warned that specialisation should not mean that the FWA divested itself of 'hopeless' cases. If only treatable cases were taken then the role of 'friend to the friendless' would be lost. However, the new casework methods depended on careful selection and, while there were no uniform procedures during the 1950s, the Association worked hard to systematise this aspect of its work during the 1960s.

By the end of the 1950s, casework had become synonymous with social work among leaders of the profession and the FWA's definition of the term had become considerably more fluent. In 1959, the provision of a casework service for people with personal and family problems became the first object of the Association. The FWA offered a definition of casework to the Ingleby Committee on Children and Young Persons (Cmnd 1191, 1960) that asserted family casework to be essentially 'relationship therapy'.[25] The principles of casework – chiefly, a belief in the worth of individuals and their right to self-determination, and belief that, given favourable conditions, an individual can grow in maturity – were also more firmly articulated. The Association also began to argue that casework was preventive. As early as 1958, the Association undertook an experimental project to see how far casework could be used preventively with discharged hospital patients deemed to have continuing social prob-

lems, albeit that it proved extremely difficult to select a sample. In the
end the organisation settled on anyone who had not previously had
casework and whom the hospital almoner felt 'would benefit' (FWA,
1961, p. 16). Whether such a definition could test the preventive properties of casework was exceedingly doubtful, but the agency was seeking
to make a contribution in a field that was to be highlighted by successive
government inquiries. (The perils for social work as a profession of
pursuing prevention had been accurately forecast as early as 1953 by
Keith-Lucas in terms of the contradiction between the injunction to apply
casework everywhere and to everyone and the limited resources available.) Muriel Cunliffe summarised both the process of casework and its
principles in her 1960 report of the review she carried out for the FWA,
which was accepted by the Association.

The FWA's growing commitment to the new casework was in part a
result of its own experiments in the field and in part a result of the
growing penetration of American ideas into British social work. In
particular, Eileen Younghusband's generic social work course begun at
the LSE in 1954 was influential in seeking to unify social work around
the concept of casework, a method hitherto used only by family caseworkers and psychiatric social workers, albeit that the 70 per cent of
the latter who worked in hospitals were, in the view of Noel Timms,
more likely to be regarded by the medical profession as social service
technicians whose role was to save the doctor time (Timms, 1964).
Younghusband brought Charlotte Towle from the University of
Chicago to assist in setting up the course. Within American social
work, Towle could not be considered to rank among those committed to
exclusively psychodynamically based social work (Rothman, 1985).
She advocated that social work give due emphasis to environment as
well as to personality, and to social reform as well as to personal
growth. However, within the British context the importance she attached to psychology was significant. In a book published by the FWA
after her British visit, she stated that 'there are no more important
courses in the professional curriculum than those in psychology' (Towle,
1956, p. 49). In an appreciation of Charlotte Towle, Helen Harris Perlman
suggested that Towle believed that all casework – that is social work –
students should be inducted into 'the psychosocial forces and mysteries
governing everyday life' (Perlman, 1969, p. 196). Younghusband sought
to link Towle to the British tradition via Octavia Hill and the development of the understanding of personal social work (Foreword to Towle,
1956).

The LSE generic course represented an attempt to universalise the casework method across social work settings, relying on a conceptualisation of casework as a *professional* relationship between client and worker that was no longer class-related. This also involved a bid to make social work something more than a residual activity defined in relation to state social services. The American writers were not afraid to assert that casework was a service needed by everyone, not just those who were unable to take advantage of welfare services. These claims were to become the basis for subsequent efforts dramatically to expand the practice of social work, which, in theory, placed the FWA in a strong position. While the Association's practice of the new casework was hardly strong in the 1950s, it was recognisably more advanced than most other places. Furthermore, the Association held a strong position in regard to the training of social workers, including those on the LSE course. In 1959, the Younghusband report for the Ministry of Health on local authority social workers not only recommended a huge increase in the numbers of social workers, but accepted the centrality of the social casework method, suggesting that the focus of statutory social work should be the social and personal needs of the family, rather than a particular aspect of the problem. In an article published in *Social Work* in 1960, Younghusband referred to the FWA's 'dizzying success' (p. 2) in persuading her working party of the value of the family casework method.

## CRITICISMS OF THE NEW CASEWORK

However, at the very moment when the new casework seemed to have achieved a position of strength, there was also evidence of a strong groundswell of opposition to it which has arguably never disappeared. Within Eileen Younghusband's Department at the LSE, Professor Richard Titmuss supported the idea of a generic social work course, but with a quite different definition of 'generic' in mind. Titmuss's preoccupation was with the need for the administrative unification of social services. In his analysis, once it had been agreed in the 1940s to abolish the poor law, a division of labour was necessary, but it had taken place according to no firm principle. Separating the individual from the mass was necessary, but reinstating the individual in the social group and the family had never happened because of *ad hoc* specialisation (Titmuss, 1954). Unifying social work was one way of tackling this problem, as it was for David Donnison after his study of the fragmentation of services for children (Donnison, 1954).

But this did not mean that Titmuss was sympathetic to the idea of a generic casework method. He was critical of what he viewed as the Family Discussion Bureau's 'passive' interviewing, with 'no minimum of essential fact', no advice or help and no follow-up.[26] In a talk he gave in New York in 1957, Titmuss was scathing about 'the preoccupation with some of the wastelands of technique' and warned of the dangers of specialisation by factual content and training in methods. Like another professor of social administration, T.S. Simey, he condemned the 'cult of supervision',[27] which he felt amounted to professionalism without the necessary interest in administration, and which for Simey lacked any scientific rigour: 'It is easy for them [social workers] to withdraw from contact with social scientists, and critical members of other professions, and to develop the practice and teaching of social work as a "mystique", carried on in secret, and handed down from generation to generation as a verbal tradition' (Simey, 1956–7, p. 113). Certainly, Kay McDougall, a lecturer at the LSE, and Una Cormack, an FWA social worker, asserted that casework was predominantly an art and could only partially be taught (McDougall and Cormack, 1954).

Titmuss believed that the effort to professionalise social work on the basis of the casework method was class-related: social workers were predominantly middle-class and welfare administrators lower middle- and working-class. But the divisions were also gender-based. While there were professional conflicts between women social workers (for example, the psychiatric social workers and the almoners voiced opposition to Younghusband's generic course), the extent to which the 'psychologising' of social work was led by female leaders of social work and, within the academic community, opposed by male social administrators is striking.

In the British context psychodynamically oriented social work was likely to be criticised for being too individualistic and for being in danger of becoming divorced from social reform. In the USA, the practice of social work was consistently linked to the development of a democratic society in that it helped to ensure that each individual realised his maximum potential. Charlotte Towle regarded casework 'as a sustaining force within an imperfectly realized democracy' (Perlman, 1969, p. 231). British caseworkers took up this theme. Cherry Morris believed that by its individual approach casework was 'one of the means of reconciling these rival claims of welfare and freedom' in a democratic society (Morris, 1954, p. 11) and Sidney Briskin, an FWA social worker, felt that the principle of acceptance derived from psychoanalysis reinforced 'the finest democratic and religious values' (Briskin, 1958, p. 523). But in the USA a political scientist pointed out the tensions between social work principles and practice, in particular that between the commitment to client self-determination and the goal of 'adjusting' the client to 'reality' (Keith-Lucas, 1953). This article was cited by Simey and passed by Simey to Titmuss, who obviously found it convincing. Social administrators were concerned that social work was becoming increasingly inward-looking, suffering from 'knowledge out of context', as Titmuss put it.[28] By focusing ever more intently on the internal world of the client, it was in danger of ignoring both wider social problems and administrative realities, which would in turn impede professionalisation. Some went further and argued that social workers were actually misinterpreting the whole nature of the client's difficulties.

This was the basis for Baroness Wootton's famous attack on social work published in 1959, the same year that the Younghusband Report recommended a huge increase in the number of social workers. In Barbara Wootton's view the 'maladjusted' had 'taken the place formerly reserved for the poor in the ideology of social work' (Wootton, 1959, p.269). She was particularly critical of family caseworkers in this regard because most of their clients were poor. In her view, economic problems were still being confused with personal failure, but in the name of personality rather than character. As she pointed out, the judgement 'unable to benefit from therapy' resonated with earlier designations of 'unhelpable' (Wootton, 1959, p. 192). Charity had been exchanged for psychology, which had resulted in an increase in courtesy on the part of the social worker towards the client, but at the price of a 'fantastically pretentious facade' (ibid., p. 271). Wootton mocked the idea of the casework relationship, commenting that the social worker's best hope of realising it lay in marrying her client, and argued that the notion of a 'professional relationship' between worker and client was a chimera. Class superiority remained alive and well, and the social worker 'knew best' (Wootton, 1959b). Wootton therefore concluded that social workers should not probe behind the presenting difficulty, but rather offer practical help that did not require 'insight' (Wootton, 1959; Wootton, 1960). Wootton admired the large amount of practical social work that was revealed by Barbara Rodgers and Julia

Dixon's observation of social work in a northern town (Rodgers and Dixon, 1960).

Thus Wootton condemned both the theory of the new casework and the efforts to professionalise social work on the back of it. Robin Huws Jones, who sat on the Younghusband Committee and became the first principal of the National Institute of Social Work, believed that Wootton was actually attacking what British social work might become if it continued to travel down the American path.[29] It is doubtful whether Wootton's idea of social work as commonsense practical help and the coordination of services amounted to a profession. She believed that ideally social work should be 'self-liquidating', which went far beyond the criticisms of other social administrators. The plethora of post-war reports on various branches of social work that preceded the 1959 Younghusband Report all recommended an increase in the numbers of social workers,[30] not out of a commitment to the practice of casework, but in recognition of the fact that complex welfare systems required mediators. It was also recognised that Wootton's wish to divorce practical help from moral judgement was not possible, although unfortunately the psychological jargon of adjustment often served to obscure the problem of values (Emmett, 1962).

At the end of the day Wootton probably believed that money was enough, but it had long been the basis of the FWA's creed that it was not. The COS had insisted that it took a long period of patient visiting to secure the habits necessary for self-maintenance, whether in the form of thrift, household management or regular attendance at work. However, whether every problem of rent arrears could be attributed to a 'deeper' problem of relationships was another matter. Wootton's approach offered little to the mentally ill, the abused child or the bereaved, yet the criticisms she pinpointed so powerfully refused to go away. The largeness of the claims made by the caseworker, the issue of 'social control' versus individual rights, and whether a client's problems were located more in the outer or the inner world continued to be a focus of attack for both the political left and right. To the 1970s left-wing radicals, psychodynamic social work was irrelevant. To the right-wing radicals of the 1980s, it was an indulgence.

# THE COMMITMENT TO CASEWORK IN A CHANGING WORLD OF SOCIAL WORK

Nevertheless, in 1960, the FWA had as much reason to be confident about the future of casework as not. The Younghusband report proposed three tiers of social workers for local authorities with the top tier identified firmly as qualified caseworkers. This followed the distinction made by the Tavistock Clinic in its evidence to the working party between professional caseworkers and social workers, who might be trained or untrained.[31] Caseworkers would take clients who needed 'skilled assistance' in resolving their problems (Ministry of Health, 1959, paras 7, 638). At the time of the Report, 89 per cent of social workers in local authorities had no qualifications. Younghusband was clear in her own mind that social work could be a unified profession: otherwise there was no reason why piecemeal, specialised development should not continue.[32] The working party was set up with a view to addressing the problem of administrative fragmentation[33] and in a sense its report bridged the gap between the psychological and administrative meanings of casework. Both sides in that debate could draw comfort from it. The report ignored medical arguments favouring the health visitor over the social worker,[34] and insisted upon a social work response that would vary according to client need rather than setting. And while it firmly delimited the work of welfare assistants from that of both social workers with a general training and the university-trained caseworker, it acknowledged the predominance of the new casework in dealing with all kinds of clients with complex difficulties.

Parliament welcomed the report, although, in the House of Lords debate, Barbara Wootton deplored the idea that psychological training was necessary for any but mental health workers.[35] It was in fact noteworthy that their Lordships welcomed the idea of an expansion in the numbers of social workers while at the same time making it obvious that many did not know what social workers did. This was not dissimilar to the 1947 debate that resulted in the giving of a Home Office grant to the Marriage Guidance Councils and to the FWA for the Family Discussion Bureaux, when the notion of marriage guidance was broadly welcomed as 'a good thing' without the House having any clear idea about its practice (Lewis *et al.* 1992).

The FWA also welcomed the commitment of the report to genericism and what it described as the realistic effort to staff social services with grades of worker appropriate to their function.[36] The Association was

anxious to preserve its place as a training agency and was reassured by
the position accorded casework. However, the Younghusband Report
clearly recommended the extension of casework practice to the statutory sector, which represented a significant shift away from the late
1940s belief that casework was properly the province of the voluntary
sector. The working party had been careful to ask the National Council
of Family Casework Agencies whether there was any evidence to support the idea that family casework required a voluntary setting and, in
reply, the Council's vice-chairman had said that there was no reason
why the service should not be offered by the local authority.[37] The
professionalisation of social work on the basis of the new casework
was thus something of a mixed blessing from the FWA's point of view.
On the one hand, it confirmed the agency's position as a leader in the
field of social work, but, on the other, by extending the territory of
casework it introduced a competitor. This was all the more problematic
because, as Younghusband pointed out, while the agency had convinced the working party as to the merits of casework, it had failed to
convince the public (Younghusband, 1960). The FWA did not attract
large quantities of donations. The Family Service Units were more
successful than the FWA in fund-raising in the immediate post-war
decades, probably because they were perceived as giving practical help
and, in the early phase of their existence, admitted to being amateurs
(Stephens, 1946). To this extent, it seems that the general public may
have shared Wootton's suspicion of psychodynamic, professional social work. In addition, only 4 per cent of local authorities used casework agencies at the end of the 1950s, so that it was by no means clear
as to where the FWA might look for financial support for what was
going to become an increasingly intensive, sophisticated and expensive
professional service.

Muriel Cunliffe's review of the structure and work of the FWA was
prompted in part by the work of the Younghusband working party and
her report put a lot of emphasis on the need for the FWA to liaise with
local authorities. She urged the FWA to see the involvement of local
authorities in casework as liberating, in that it would permit a 'release
from certain responsibilities', and was adamant in her view that the
FWA had to become more outward-looking.[38] As a North American,
Cunliffe was convinced that casework could and should be practised in
any setting (Cunliffe, 1960). What the FWA had to do was to unify
behind the banner of casework and make sure it retained its position in
the vanguard of training and good practice. To this end, the report made

a number of criticisms regarding the variability of practice in the Association, for example in regard to the different intake policies operating in each of the seven areas.

The FWA accepted the report and moved to strengthen its casework. Paddy Daniel, the casework consultant appointed in 1963, was effectively the head of a department and the areas worked to her in the manner recommended by Cunliffe. Both Daniel and the Casework Advisory Committee commanded considerable professional respect during the 1960s, a decade in which the dominance of casework was confirmed within social work and jealousies between caseworker and non-caseworker were powerful within some branches of social work such as probation. Within the FWA, the tensions between the professional staff and lay area committee members were if anything higher by the end of the decade than they had been during the 1950s. In a collection of papers put together by the social work staff in 1969, Pat Thomas, a principal social worker and the director of the Association from 1973 to 1976, complained that committee members were insufficiently informed about the work done by the casework staff.[39] Paddy Daniel, in her address to the FWA's Centenary Conference in 1969, stated baldly that the Association's caseworkers were professionals, but its administrators and managers were not.[40] In Thomas's view the social work department was powerful because of the work that it did and the respect it commanded in the social work field, but it had not been 'wholly accepted' by the voluntary committee members. Furthermore, it had nothing in common with FWA's other departments, devoted to the production of the *Charities Register and Digest*, dealing with inquiries about charities, the administration of trusts, pension funds, old people's homes and almshouses, and the running of the CAB.

There was in fact little holding the FWA together in the 1960s. Astbury retired from the post of secretary in 1956 and he was probably the last head of the Association to have been familiar with its different empires. While a caseworker, he had begun his career in the FWA in the Enquiry Department, which in the days of the COS had spearheaded the Society's attack on mendicity, and had turned this into the Information Department and the National Casework Department (which dealt with enquiries from outside London where there was no casework service). J.S. Burt, who as director steered the Association through the 1960s, was an administrator unfamiliar with casework, and this served to exacerbate the fundamental divide between caseworkers and the rest within the organisation. Thus, during the period of its greatest prestige as a casework agency, the FWA was nevertheless fragile. Cunliffe had pointed out that the area staff remained rather small for the successful delivery of a professional casework service, and that financial support for casework remained a problem. Whereas four of 11 Family Service Units received 100 per cent funding from the local authorities,[41] the FWA never achieved more than 75 per cent and, after the formation of the London boroughs in 1965, Labour-controlled councils such as Tower Hamlets tended to be suspicious of charity in general and of the FWA in particular. At the end of the decade the FWA faced a further convulsion in terms of its relationship with statutory social work in the form of the Seebohm proposals for unified social services departments and an internal crisis that was sparked both by lack of clarity regarding direction and by lack of money.

## NOTES

1.  'Notes on the Oxford Conference', *Social Work*, 2, October, 1941, p. 54.
2.  Memo of an interview with representatives of the senior Secretaries Group, 30 July 1942, A/FWA/C/A21/1, f. 31, FWA Papers, Greater London Record Office.
3.  Standing Sub-Committee on Family Allowances, 16 December 1942, A/FWA/C/A19/1, f. 107.
4.  Memo of an interview with Eileen Younghusband, 14 September 1942, A/FWA/C/A21/1, f. 58.
5.  Letter from Cherry Morris, *Social Work*, 2, July, 1943, pp. 357–9.
6.  See above, pp. 87–8.
7.  Memorandum by Miss Lawrence, 15 December 1947, A/FWA/C/A19/1, f. 163.
8.  PRO, CAB 87/82, SIC (42) 168, COS 'Training in Social Work', 15 October 1942.
9.  'Principles of Family Case Work', 1943, A/FWA/C/A21/1, f. 102.
10. Minutes of the Aims and Policy Committee, November 1949, A/FWA/C/A19/1, f. 200.
11. Draft Report from the Central Committee on Aims and Policy, A/FWA/C/A7/1, f. 296.
12. Minutes of the Administrative Council, 4 June 1953, A/FWA/C/A7/1, f. 294.
13. Dame Enid Russell Smith, Note for Discussion, 'Training for Social Work – How we might proceed', 2 July 1953, PRO, MH 130/7.
14. Memo by Mrs Eicholz on the work of the Marriage Welfare Sub-Committee, 14 October 1948, A/FWA/C/A3/66.
15. Report of the Marriage Welfare Sub-Committee of the FWA to the end of November 1948, PRO, HO 45/25203.
16. Memo by A.T.M. Wilson, June 1948, PRO, HO 45/25203.
17. P. Boys Smith, Minute on the FWA, 6 December 1949, PRO, HO 45/25203.
18. 'Family Discussion Bureaux', November 1953, A/FWA/C/A7/2, f. 50.
19. 'Problem Families', 5 February 1948, A/FWA/C/A19/1, ff. 157–8.
20. Minutes of the Sub-Committee on Problem Families, 23 June 1947, ibid., f. 150.
21. 'Report to the Carnegie Trust on the Problem Families Project', n.d., A/FWA/C/A7/1, f. 150.

22. 'Report to the Administrative Council from the Problem Families Sub-Committee', 5 November 1952, A/FWA/C/A7/1, ff. 226–7.

23. Minutes of the Administrative Committee, Consideration of the FWA/Tavistock Relationship, 27 January 1949, A/FWA/C/A3/66.

24. Draft Report from the Central Committee on Aims and Policy, March 1953, A/FWA/C/A7/1, f. 299.

25. Minutes of the Administrative Council, Evidence to the Ingleby Committee, 7 November 1957, A/FWA/C/A7/3/1, ff. 91–2.

26. Marginalia on FWA, 'Memo on post-graduate training for caseworkers in "marriage guidance" Centres', 1950, Titmuss Papers, Box 405, BLPES, LSE.

27. R.M. Titmuss, 'Social Policy and Social Work Education', 1957 TS, Titmuss Papers, Box 300 C.

28. Titmuss, 'Social Policy and Social Work Education'.

29. Robin Huws Jones to Eileen Younghusband, 22 February 1960, Younghusband Papers, Correspondence, P 1844, National Institute of Social Work. (These papers have been catalogued but there are a number of discrepancies between the handlist and content of the boxes. References refer to the boxes.)

30. The Mackintosh Committee (Cmd 8260, 1951) on mental health workers; the Cope Committee (Cmd 8188, 1951) on almoners (termed medical auxiliaries); the Underwood Committee (Ministry of Education, 1955) on maladjusted children and child guidance; and the Albermarle Committee (Cmd 929, 1960) on the youth service.

31. Evidence of the Tavistock Clinic to the Younghusband Working Party, n.d., Younghusband Papers, C2/83.

32. 'Professional Social Work and the Report of the Working Party on Social Workers', draft notes for a talk, circa 1959, Younghusband Papers, C2/98.

33. Geraldine Aves to Enid Russell Smith, 9 June 1952, PRO, MH 130/7. This was also the motivating factor for the Joint Universities Committee for Social Studies and Public Administration; see Notes of a Meeting between the HO, MH and JUC, 4 December 1953, ibid.

34. For example, that of the Medical Officer of Health for the LCC, J.A. Scott, 'Social Workers and the Local Health and Welfare Authorities', Younghusband Papers, C2/45.

35. House of Lords, Debates, 17 February 1960, c. 104.

36. Comments to the Ministry of Health on the Younghusband Report, 12 October 1959, A/FWA/C/A14/1/1, f. 157.

37. Oral Evidence of the National Council of Family Casework Agencies, Association of General and Family Caseworkers and Liverpool Personal Service Society, 23 November 1956, Younghusband Papers, C1/39.

38. Muriel Cunliffe, *A Report of the Review of the FWA*, 1960, pp. 21–2, TS, FWA Archives, Dalston.

39. Pat Thomas, 'Letter from Principal to Chairman, Area 6', in FWA, *A Collection of Papers by Members of the Social Work Staff*, 1969, TS, FWA Archives, Dalston.

40. M.P. Daniel, 'Changes and Prospects in the Aims and Methods of Social Work, and the Place of the Volunteer Element in the System', Address to the FWA Centenary Conference, 1969, A/FWA/C/C18/11.

41. Evidence of the FSU to the Younghusband Working Party, n.d., Younghusband Papers, A1/13.

# 6.   Purpose and provenance, 1970–90

The creation of unified social services departments in 1970, two years after the publication of the Seebohm report, highlighted the problem the FWA faced in carving out a space for itself as a voluntary casework agency in relation to local authority-based social work at a time of particularly acute financial crisis. Having identified itself as primarily a casework agency after the Cunliffe report, the Association found the cost of casework increasingly hard to support.

The convulsions of the Association during the early 1970s can only be explained in terms of the interplay between the organisation's environment and its internal divisions. The latter were long-standing. The 'burden of history' was heavier for the FWA than for many voluntary organisations, in terms of both its public image and the apparent lack of connection between its parts once the COS's philosophy of charity had given way to, on the one hand, a more pragmatic view of the possibility of a complementary 'partnership' between the statutory and voluntary sector and, on the other, a professional approach to casework. Casework came to be seen more as an end in itself than as a means to achieving social change. During the 1960s the FWA had committed itself to becoming a fully professional casework agency, but it was run at the local level by lay committees who were not wholly convinced by the canons of psychodynamic social work, and at the central level by administrators whose professional culture was often closer to the other elements of the organisation's work. The financial crisis of the early 1970s exacerbated these conflicts.

After the setting up of local authority social services departments (SSDs), the FWA found itself playing a supplementary rather than a complementary role in relation to the statutory services, which did not make it any easier to justify its warranting state funding. The Association had a method – casework – in which it continued to excel, but it had no clear client group. Having operated alongside the state on the basis of, first, a separation of spheres and client groups and, later on, a separation of tasks, the organisation was no longer able to lay claim to either. Nor could the Association count on the prestige it had wielded during the 1960s, in part because the business of training social workers had become much bigger with the creation of the Central Council for Education and Training in Social Work, and in part because casework itself came under renewed attack, both from a new school of radical social work which emphasised the importance of environment over personality and, more pragmatically, in the new SSDs from the pressure of huge caseloads. The FWA continued to appear attractive to many social workers, but because of its better working conditions as much as, or more than, its place in the vanguard of casework theory and practice.

At the end of the 1970s, the FWA found itself being required to adjust to another set of shifts in government policy, this time directly addressing the relationship between statutory and voluntary provision. The new Conservative administration of 1979 talked about restoring 'Victorian values' and about its desire to roll back state social provision in favour of the market, the family and the voluntary sector. As had proved the case with the professionalisation of social work on the basis of casework, this presented both opportunity and pitfall. The possibility of expansion was held out, but the long-standing problems of goals, governance, organisational structure and financial security were papered over rather than resolved and at the end of the decade the bubble burst again. In common with the voluntary sector generally, the FWA faced a rapidly escalating pace of change during the 1980s which proved extremely hard to manage. From the complementary/supplementary relationships which had begun to characterise the voluntary/statutory partnership during the inter-war period and which matured during the years of the classic welfare state, voluntary organisations were invited to become more entrepreneurial. This in turn required a more corporate culture, something that was perhaps particularly hard for a psychodynamic social work agency successfully to achieve.

## THE FWA AND THE NEW SOCIAL SERVICES DEPARTMENTS

The Seebohm Committee on Local Authority and Allied Personal Social Services was set up in 1965 to review the organisation of responsibilities of the local authority personal social services[1] and to consider what changes were desirable to secure an effective family service. The

process by which the search for a unified family service became the
final step towards a reorganisation designed to secure the unification of
social work has been described by Hall (1976) and Cooper (1983). In a
sense, the Seebohm proposals represented the culmination of the social
administrators' determination to use the concept of generic social work
to overcome fragmentation of the personal social services,[2] together
with their more general faith in the power of an administrative reorganisation – 'a technical fix' – to achieve a change in principle and
purpose. Richard Titmuss played a key role in leading the group that
had called for a committee of inquiry and, together with Professor J.N.
Morris, the only medical member of the Committee, made the linkages
between the reform of the personal social services and health service
reorganisation (Lewis, 1986).

Expressing optimism about the preventive properties of social work,
the Seebohm Report (Cmnd 3703, 1968) aimed to make social work
accessible to all families and to create unified social work departments. In principle, then, it tended towards universality and genericism.
Many members of the Committee were certainly committed to universality. Robin Huws Jones, who had been the vice-chairman of the
Younghusband working party and who was a member of the Seebohm
Committee, was convinced both that social services should be provided
on the basis of citizenship entitlement and that uptake of the social
services was percolating upwards through the social classes.[3] However,
while the latter point may have been true of much social provision, it
did not apply to the personal social services. More important, it is not
clear whether the Committee made a connection between the creation
of a unified service that was universal rather than for families and the
implications of universal access for the practice of social work. When
Baroness Serota, also a member of the Seebohm Committee, delivered
the fourth Eileen Younghusband Lecture at the National Institute of
Social Work Training in 1970, she argued that the unification of social
work was necessary to establish the principle of universality and to
eradicate stigma.[4] This was a pipe-dream, in that the personal social
services remained highly residual, but the creation of a single-door
service nevertheless had the effect of dramatically increasing the numbers of clients.

The principle of genericism proved notoriously ambiguous. The Committee recommended that the basic field social worker should move
towards taking responsibility 'for the whole range of individual and
family social problems, drawing on support in this from consultants

within the social services department' (Cmnd 3703,1968, para.18), which made it sound as though the basic grade social worker would be expected to deal with the whole gamut of presenting problems, calling on the help of specialists in the department. However, later on in the report, the Committee recommended that 'nevertheless subject to certain provisos ... we consider that a family or individual in need of social care should, as far as possible, be served by a single social worker' (ibid., para. 516), which made it sound more as though one worker was intended to take responsibility for a client, but that a range of workers might be involved in providing care.[5] What is striking is the lack of attention paid by the Committee to defining the role and tasks of social workers compared to the attention paid the structures necessary for service delivery. This may be seen as further evidence of the Committee's preoccupation with genericism as a means to achieving administrative unification. Certainly Titmuss would not have wished the Committee to give support to the idea of genericism in terms of the casework method. During the 1960s there is evidence that he was attracted by the role social work could play in community development, the theoretical implications underlying which he considered to be 'of the greatest importance, since they imply that welfare can be developed by the utilisation of a process of rational planning'.[6] In some measure the Seebohm Committee replaced the concept of family with that of community (Cooper, 1983) and was enthusiastic about social workers developing the conditions favourable to community identity and activity, but the clear delineation of roles that had characterised the 1959 Younghusband report was missing. Social workers themselves were on the whole too entranced by the prospect of controlling and developing their own social services departments to offer any criticism, but a few expressed anxiety about the control that would be given local authorities in setting standards, and about the pace of change (Stevenson, 1968) in a situation when 80 per cent of local authorities social workers were still untrained (Hall, 1976).

The problems all this raised for a voluntary casework agency were legion. The Seebohm Committee explicitly addressed the role of the voluntary sector in its report, noting the pioneering role voluntary organisations had played historically and suggesting that they would continue to have a major role 'developing citizen participation in revealing new needs and in exposing shortcomings in the services' (Cmnd 3703, para. 495). The Committee thus offered the voluntary sector the role of pioneer and watchdog, and warned local authorities that they would have to tolerate criticism. The Committee's attachment to the idea of community also prompted it to urge local authorities to encourage volunteering and to include volunteers in its plans. When Sir Frederic Seebohm addressed the Annual General Meeting of the FWA in 1968 he again stressed the part voluntary organisations could and should play in experimentation and in providing additional client choice (something that Younghusband also acknowledged that she had come to accept[7]), but he warned that they would have to re-examine attitudes and be prepared to undergo change.[8]

The FWA offered a defence of its work in the evidence it gave to the Seebohm Committee in terms of its position as a pioneer in the field of casework and as a provider of a flexible service that supplemented those of the local authorities.[9] In making the latter point the organisation was breaking new ground: prior to 1970 local authorities had certainly viewed the FWA as a complementary provider.[10] The agency could claim to offer a unique system of casework supervision and low caseloads that ensured the client time to resolve his problems; it also tried to lay some claim to preventive work. The FWA was in greater difficulty when it came to Seebohm's two main principles, universality and genericism. The Association offered a professional service. While it might pioneer innovations in that service, its task was essentially to sell a supplementary service and the buyer was increasingly local government. All the increase in the Association's funding during the 1950s came from the local authorities. But now that the new SSDs were to be accessible to all the job of persuading local government that the FWA was worth supporting became logically harder. The interpretation of 'generic' also raised difficulties. The FWA had built its post-war reputation on its development of a skilled, specialised casework service. The new social work environment might reject this as old-fashioned.

## INTERNAL CRISIS

By the early 1970s, the FWA was running a substantial deficit of some £38 000. A report made to members following the 1971 annual general meeting attributed this to a falling away of legacies, donations and subscriptions and to an increase in overheads due mainly to the costs of casework.[11] Eileen Younghusband pointed out in an address to the 1973 annual general meeting of the FWA's Area 4 that the Association ranked 99th out of the top 100 fund-raising charities.[12] The crisis faced by the

FWA in the early 1970s was not only financial. At one of a series of extraordinary general meetings called in 1971, a member charged that the fundamental problems were ones of policy rather than finance. Local authority social services had undergone huge change, but the FWA appeared static.[13] As is so often the case in voluntary organisations, financial crisis brought other underlying problems into focus. In the case of the FWA, this proved particularly divisive because both issues of purpose and structure related so strongly to the position of casework within the agency, which was also the department with the highest burden of debt.

After a series of very short-serving directors and acting directors – four in the space of one year – and a disastrous centenary year fundraising campaign, Janet Lacey was brought in from the Christian Aid to serve as acting director and was persuaded to stay until 1973. Lacey was sought because of her administrative skills and on her arrival she immediately identified the lack of cohesion in the Association. There was, she felt, a lack of communication between departments, and between the central and local offices; each department had a budget, but there was no ready means of calling a halt to spending; and each department and area made decisions but there was no means of acting upon them.[14] In many respects Lacey was merely setting out clearly the problems of 'separate empires' that had plagued the Association for some considerable time. Members of particular departments tended to identify with those departments rather than with FWA as an organisation.

As an administrator, Lacey disliked the power wielded by the caseworkers within the organisation and their apparent lack of financial accountability. Caseworkers tended to take the view that their job as professionals was to deliver the casework service and not to worry about the financial deficit.[15] Lacey made it clear that there was not enough money to pay for specialist, in-depth casework unless the local authorities could be persuaded to increase their financial support, and was irritated by caseworker insouciance about money. On arrival she asked for £20 000 of savings, £15 000 from the casework department, which prompted the resignation of the casework consultant, Paddy Daniel.[16] But her antipathy to casework seemed to go deeper than the financial problems it represented for the organisation. In her contribution to the annual report for 1969–70 her reference to the fact that many people were hesitant about having their problems examined by social workers seemed to hark back to the views of Barbara Wootton. She was more outspoken in a paper she prepared for the board of management she set up in 1970: 'It would appear that, with a "closed shop" profession the chance of being creative in the widest sense of the word is a remote possibility.'[17]

The caseworkers themselves certainly interpreted her position towards them as hostile. Pat Thomas, then a caseworker in Lewisham, resigned at the end of 1970 after a series of acrimonious struggles with Lacey; it is of course significant that she returned to head the Association in 1973. Writing of Lacey as a client coming to an intake interview, Thomas described her as 'a difficult personality whose behaviour shows a high degree of confusion, much splitting and projection, a need for power'. She went on to add: 'If the client finds the parent body unable to give help and recognition, it may have to prepare to become independent.'[18] Given the long-term difficulties of the casework service in raising funds, this was nothing more than a pious hope. Lacey's impatience with the caseworkers' lack of financial realism was not unfounded. However, her handling of what was a very difficult situation proved little short of disastrous.

In the first place, there was a genuine and unfortunate clash of cultures between a director who was inclined to hierarchy and authoritarianism and a social work department that was inward-looking and used to considerable autonomy. Second, the director's decision to take a top-down managerial approach jarred in a participative organisation with a tradition of strong input from its Council and relatively open management. Third, Lacey did not direct very well. On her arrival she deplored the fact that there were no fewer than 29 overlapping committees and commented that 'the trouble with the present Constitution is that it seems to have been devised on the assumption that FWA was entirely concerned with professional social casework and, what is more important, that it is more suitable for a coordinating body than for an operational Association'.[19] In a letter to Pat Thomas, Lacey asserted that 'the discussions on something called "democracy" are irrelevant in our present situation'.[20] Her appointment of an undemocratic board of management aroused huge discontent and resulted in a series of successful moves at the annual and extraordinary general meetings of 1971 to establish a study group composed largely of outsiders and chaired by David Hobman, who had just revamped Age Concern, to review the position of the agency. A second working party produced a new constitution for the Association and the job description for Pat Thomas who succeeded Janet Lacey.

Lacey's taste for secrecy and authoritarian direction fuelled the suspicions and divisions within FWA. She asked the Christian Organisations Research and Advisory Trust (CORAT) to review the position of FWA,[21] and repeatedly promised that large-scale change would follow in the wake of its report. However, she then suppressed the report when it appeared in 1970. Caseworkers like Valerie Kelly, who also resigned at the beginning of 1971, believed that the director did 'not want to give priority to personal social service by professional social workers' and saw the secrecy surrounding both the board of management and the CORAT report as evidence of a conspiracy against social work.[22] Pat Thomas, on the other hand, speculated that the CORAT report was quashed because it made favourable references to casework.[23] In fact, as Lacey acknowledged to a meeting of one of the area committees, and more eliptically to a 1970 extraordinary general meeting, she suppressed the report because she felt that it was insufficiently radical on the questions of finance and structure; in other words it did not provide her with the ammunition to appoint a board of management.[24] The CORAT report was certainly bland and unhelpful, but suppressing it lowered morale in the organisation and stoked up the rumours among the caseworkers, whose stock-in-trade was to look for and be sensitive to hidden meanings.

The board of management was also responsible for some arbitrary decisions, which caused uproar in an organisation used to consultation and where relationships between the areas and the central bodies had been historically fragile. In particular, the decision in 1971 to close down Area 3 (Hackney) prompted an outcry at the extraordinary general meeting held at the end of the year. Mr W. Harbert, the Director of Hackney Social Services Department and member of the board of management, blamed the social workers for not being willing to add to the activities of the Family Centre in order to attract more funding from the borough.[25] The local authority had asked the Association to provide services for the mentally ill and for handicapped children, which the casework consultant said fell outside the FWA's concern to work with family relationships. This episode was a harbinger of things to come. As Lacey asked the directors of the ten Inner London Boroughs for 100 per cent funding for the casework service, so the Association was obliged to reconsider what it was prepared to provide. Lacey seemed to have a vague idea about the FWA's social workers providing a community service; she spoke of casework being more useful if the 'caseworkers were operating in a wider framework'.[26] But whether this amounted to putting the emphasis on community development rather than case-work, or merely responding more positively to local authority demands was never clear. Mr Harbert resigned from the board in the middle of 1970, declaring himself unwilling to face any more extraordinary general meetings.[27]

The study group was set up ostensibly to look at social work within the Association in the context of the Seebohm reforms. In Harbert's view, which he made public in an article published in the *British Hospital Journal and Social Services Review*, the group's intention was to curb the activities of the board of management and 'like so many FWA committees, it under-represents the money-getters and over-represents the spenders' (Harbert, 1972, p. 137). By this he probably meant that the group was weighted towards the caseworkers' view. Its members included a recently retired assistant principal probation officer, three academics, the director of training for the London Boroughs Training Committee, the chairman of Area 4 and the casework consultant. Harbert warned that 'the only possible road to survival for the family casework service is through projects which will attract funds – research, innovation and experimental work' (ibid.). The group's report, issued at the beginning of 1972, certainly paid little attention to the question of finance, focusing rather on the purpose and structure of the organisation.[28] It sought a unifying concept or philosophy for the Association and, like the Cunliffe report of 1960, lamented the FWA's tendency to be inward-looking. Also like Cunliffe, it endorsed the casework focus of the organisation, but urged that casework should be more broadly interpreted in the future and looked favourably on both group and community work. The study group assumed that the FWA would continue to provide 25 per cent of the costs of the casework service, an assumption that was rapidly to prove problematic. In terms of structure, the group set out to restore democratic governance. It rejected a decentralised model such as that offered by the Family Service Units, on the grounds that the FWA needed strong leadership, but it sought to give much greater powers to the Council in order to act as a check on the director. In the new Articles of Association adopted in 1972, the main objects of the FWA were listed as the provision of casework, training in social work, research and experimental work, and the administration of trust funds. The dual nature of the FWA was thus reconfirmed once again and casework restored to pride of place, although the study group recommended that the casework consultant report to the director rather than operate entirely separately.

At the end of Lacey's directorship the FWA moved from Denison House, its home since the late nineteenth century, to less imposing and less conveniently situated quarters in Hackney. The sale raised some £300 000 which dulled the edge of financial crisis. The new regime was also faced with a *fait accompli* in terms of the decision taken by the board of management to hive off the CAB service. The London boroughs wanted to see a united service and the board of management agreed to pay the CAB an £8000 per year dowry in perpetuity (this proved a source of conflict in 1975, when the FWA again found itself facing financial difficulties and defaulted on the undertaking). In theory, the twin services of casework and advice should have reinforced each other but, as the Cunliffe report noted in 1960, only 8 per cent of the FWA's referrals came from the CAB. Nevertheless, at the time it looked as though as part of a general retrenchment (the Educational Grants Advisory Service also disappeared in 1972) the FWA was getting rid of a highly successful service.

The study group drafted the advertisement for a new director, whom it felt did not necessarily have to be a professional social worker, but must be able to understand the essence of casework practice. The casework consultant felt that the director had to be able to cope with 'anxieties' pushed up through the hierarchy and with the 'aggression' inevitably aroused by an authority figure in an organisation such as FWA, and therefore had to be a social worker.[29] The new director, Pat Thomas, was a social worker, but even she found it difficult to bring the casework department under her control.

In her final comments to Council following her letter of resignation in 1976, Thomas pointed out that she had always been in charge of two and a half organisations: social work, trusts and the half consisting of publications and information. During her term of office she had sought to give the FWA both greater unity as an organisation, making the little empires feel as though they mattered and belonged, and a stronger identity. She proposed the centralisation of social work, using the Tavistock Institute as a model, and emphasising research rather than practice. Thomas believed that social work as a profession was quite distinct from welfare work and generalised social services and that the FWA should be prepared to say so and to act as a 'professional catalyst'. She proposed calling the new centre 'The Casework Centre' or 'The National Centre for Casework Training and Treatment'.[30] However, the proposal met with strong opposition from area committees, which remained fiercely independent, and from social workers who felt a loyalty to their areas and to the local practice of casework. Thomas accepted their views and abandoned her proposal. But the problem of how to fund social work remained; the role of the area committees had not been clarified in the reorganisation of the early 1970s; the role of social work in the organisation was no clearer; and the dual nature of the whole enterprise persisted: after all the convulsions of the early 1970s, the underlying problems were unchanged in their essentials. The new Council elected in 1973 was talented and energetic and undertook important tasks, particularly in respect of modernising the administration of the trust funds (the Association managed 129 charities during the 1970s). The new Council felt that it was revitalising a body on the verge of disintegration, but in a very real sense it was only tinkering at the edges. In his final speech as chairman to the 1977 annual general meeting, Roger Martyn acknowledged that the FWA had two very different tasks, social work on the one hand and the business of grants and publishing on the other, and wondered if it might not be 'better for a charity to concentrate on one field'.[31] However, during the 1980s, FWA was further to diffuse its efforts.

## THE ROLE OF SOCIAL WORK

The study group contacted social services departments in an effort to establish where the local authorities (LAs) felt that the FWA could make a contribution. The replies indicated that directors of social services thought that the FWA should concentrate its efforts on people requiring heavy investment: the mentally handicapped, the homeless, families in danger of breakdown, rootless youngsters.[32] For the first time the FWA began to talk of the need for the organisation to 'plug the gaps'. Its focus on family casework was not sufficient to differentiate it from the new SSDs and, more to the point, many LAs were not willing to fund such a service. But the Association faced difficulties in establishing a clear identity as a voluntary organisation carrying out social work. To some extent this had always been the case. The 1960 Cunliffe report had distinguished it from the Family Service Units by the rather too neat idea that, while the FSU dealt with problem families, the FWA dealt with families who had problems. There was also some overlap with the National Marriage Guidance Council in terms of client group. The study group report showed that 40 per cent of the FWA's clients had marital problems.

During the post-war decades the FWA had built its identity around a specialist casework method. The Association dealt with relationships rather than a particular category of clients. But, as Helen Martyn pointed out in her 1973 address to the annual general meeting in Area 5, the post-Seebohm era put the organisation in a double bind: to specialise was 'old hat', but if the FWA did not then it became indistinguishable from the statutory social services.[33] Bob Morley, a trained caseworker who followed Pat Thomas as director and stayed in post until the end of the 1980s, resolved the issue by arguing that the casework method was generalisable to a variety of client groups and settings. He sought to make social work 'proactive', and to reach out to where the people in trouble were, whether in launderettes or GPs' surgeries, suggesting that psychodynamic methods did not have to be used behind closed doors.[34] This increased the activity level in the FWA, but did not necessarily provide a clearer identity.

The picture of the agency during the 1970s tended to be of an elitist organisation, treating a few clients in depth. The FWA appeared at once luxurious and insignificant in terms of its caseload. Pat Thomas in particular was anxious to keep the flag flying for unadulterated casework. However, the financial strain of providing it did not lessen. In general, the position of the FWA during the 1970s was that it was prepared to finance 25 per cent of the costs of the casework service; many in the organisation feared that 100 per cent funding from external sources would have eroded its independence. But in the mid-1970s, the borough of Tower Hamlets provided only 38 per cent of the funding necessary for the local FWA area's casework. At the end of the decade social services were referring a lower percentage of the FWA's clients (14 per cent) than they had done at the beginning of the decade, which meant that they had no great incentive to provide more funding. A borough like Islington was singled out by the 1978 Wolfenden Report on the future of voluntary organisations as providing generous support to the voluntary sector, but this was not the experience of the FWA. The reasons for social services directors' opposition to funding the FWA ranged from the ideological to the pragmatic. There was no evidence that the FWA's areas sought to adapt to the needs of a particular borough and many directors must have regarded their services as something of a luxury.

Caseloads in the FWA averaged between 15 and 20 clients, compared to the 92 in a social services department studied by Goldberg and Warburton (1979) in 1972 (by 1975, this number had been reduced to 57). The FWA operated a stringent system of supervision. The casework consultant saw the principal social workers once a fortnight in the area office and then held a case conference. One informant described the first two years of supervision as a process that 'knocked you down and built you up'. The FWA did both short- and long-term work. A significant proportion of the FWA's work (20 per cent according to the study group) continued to be related to financial problems. Many case-workers nevertheless had a preference for in-depth, long-term work, in addition to which the leverage exercised by clients in a voluntary casework organisation was quite different from that in a social services department and also tended to promote long-term work. Whereas a social services department client was likely to threaten the social worker with some form of bad behaviour, in the FWA he was more likely to threaten not to come and only the skill of the worker could hold him. The agency lost a lot of clients on referral and only accepted the motivated, but almost half the clients dropped out throughout the 1960s and 1970s.[35] The caseworkers appreciated the clinical freedom they were able to exercise.[36] The organisation was committed to the use of psychodynamic methods and ran a successful conference in 1973 on family therapy (Finn, 1974), which exuded considerable intellectual excitement. But it drew a clear line between psychoanalysis and case-work; in the latter the client benefited as much from the casework relationship as from the insight gained.[37] Compared to local authority social workers, the FWA caseworkers' role seemed admirably clear, even if that of the agency was not. They had no statutory responsibili-ties and between a third and a half were themselves engaged in psycho-therapy. From the social worker's point of view, the FWA was by all accounts an interesting and rewarding place to be.

Within the local authorities, casework was unable to withstand the bombardment of referrals after 1970, but it was difficult to find a model to replace it. Authorities experimented with intake teams, team manag-ers who monitored the flow of work, group allocation meetings and time-limited contracts with clients. The new managerialist ethos of the SSDs eroded the autonomy of social workers (Bamford, 1990). The British Association of Social Workers' 1977 statement on roles and tasks encompassed casework, group and community work and insisted that the social worker dealt with personal relations and was not a mere mobiliser of resources, but, as Parsloe (1981) pointed out, BASW's analysis of roles could not be used in practice when it became more a matter of crisis intervention and allocating clients on the basis of risk. In response to the deluge, social workers struggled to stop deskilling, frequently by informal specialisation (Stevenson and Parsloe, 1978; Challis and Ferlie, 1987), while social work academics struggled to fit theory to practice. Some used systems theories in attempts at unification and to provide basic terms of reference in relation to social work's broad objectives (Butrym, 1976; Howe, 1987); some defined social work in terms of problem solving, albeit deeply rooted in psychosocial understanding (Perlman, 1970); and others turned to the idea of 'task-centred' work, in which the problems and agenda for action were agreed between client and worker (Goldberg *et al.*, 1985). In the 1978 Loch Memorial Lecture, W.B. Utting, then Chief Social Work Officer in the DHSS, commented that SSDs did not necessarily provide an environment that encouraged the practice of social work because of their size and their focus on service delivery (Utting, 1978). Certainly, social workers in local authority departments were massively discontented by the end of the decade.

Thus, while the FWA felt threatened by the new SSDs, it could also feel superior and defend its practices in the name of 'real social work'. The study group's support for in-depth casework derived from the belief of its members in its effectiveness and its rarity in local authority social work, which made the training offered by FWA all the more valuable. Nevertheless, the prestige of casework came under attack from sources other than the hard-pressed SSDs. A highly influential study of FWA practice published by John E. Mayer and Noel Timms in 1970 had cast doubt on the effectiveness of casework. The study focused on the view of the client, something that both the Younghusband and Seebohm reports had ignored and about which Barbara Wootton (1959) had expressed considerable interest. Mayer and Timms (1970) examined the gap in expectation and understanding between client and worker and found that those clients treated by more psychodynamically inclined workers tended to be more dissatisfied. These workers tried to make clients more self aware and to give them a better understanding of their problems and how they contributed to them. Their non-interventionist approach puzzled the clients, who did not expect that they would be the focus of attention, but rather the person whom they held responsible for their difficulties. Some concluded that the social worker was not interested in helping them, some that the worker did not understand their problems, some that she had been confused by the conflicting stories she was presented with, and some that she was unable to exercise authority necessary to resolve the problems. Mayer and Timms concluded in a manner that would have infuriated Wootton, to the effect that working-class people were something of a different species when it came to problem solving and did not understand psychotherapeutic processes. But their point that in many cases social worker and client were talking past each other and its implications for judging the effectiveness of the casework method was powerful. One respondent felt that the study seriously affected the willingness of some local authorities to fund the FWA. A study of casework practice in the Family Service Units by Eric Sainsbury (1975) found much wider satisfaction among clients, although he too concluded that the clients' acceptance of an agency was related to the extent that their immediate needs were met; all but one of the FSU clients in his sample wanted and received material help as well as help with relationships.

Casework also came under attack more generally. A 1970 article by Martin Rein, an American, had talked about the need for social work to renew its commitment to social reform and condemned the focus on methods. There had been, he felt, too much emphasis on professional development and not enough on the relevance of social work to society. In 1973, Eileen Younghusband acknowledged the strength of the voices denying that social work could be equated with casework and called for social workers to work for structural change.[38] She denied that there was a dichotomous choice to be made between personality and environment, but the pendulum swung during the 1970s towards the latter (for example, Bailey and Brake, 1975). In the process the idea of personal responsibility in particular became extremely unpopular. The FWA had always stressed the importance of this, from the point of view of the national good in its early twentieth-century campaigns against state intervention and as part of personal growth and development in the post-war period. But students coming to the Association for training during the 1970s were likely to be extremely dismissive of any method that located the cause of difficulty in the individual rather than in the wider society.[39] During the 1980s, casework was also attacked from the political Right.

## TOWARDS A MORE CORPORATE CULTURE: THE 1980s

The climate for social work showed little sign of improvement during the 1980s. Social workers employed by local government had been subjected to managerial control relatively early compared to other public servants, as part of the response to the high caseloads experienced by the new SSDs. During the 1980s, managerialism, whose 'litany' has included the imposition of cash limits and performance indicators stressing economy and efficiency, staff cuts, staff appraisal, merit pay, devolved budgets, management training, new planning systems and a rhetorical emphasis on the response to the 'consumer' (Pollitt, 1993), spread throughout the public services, fuelled by the conviction that all too often public servants had served themselves first and failed the public. As the death count of children at risk mounted, social workers were subjected to a sustained attack that accused them of ideological rigidity and questioned their competence. The criticism of the professions which ran through all the efforts to reform the public sector during the 1980s was particularly harsh when it came to social work. W.B. Utting (1992) pointed out the degree to which social work's association with local government made it vulnerable. The social policing of the private sphere that local authority social workers are obliged to perform as part of their statutory duties has always placed them in a difficult position in the modern liberal state, liable to accusations of overly zealous intervention, on the one hand, and negligence, on the other. Utting also made reference to the 'anti-professional and anti-intellectual outlook of some authorities, and a management that did not understand the nature of its business' (ibid., p. 14) leading to a neglect of professional supervision. In other words, while there was something to complain about in respect of social work in the SSDs, it was not necessarily fair to blame social workers themselves.

However, in the case of social work, the criticism was not merely about how the work was done – whether it gave value for money and whether it paid due regard to the user of the services – but also about the nature of the whole activity. It was this that made the position of social workers different from that of doctors, teachers or lawyers, all of whom also came under fire, and it was this that made the position of family caseworkers in the voluntary sector vulnerable. As early as 1980, Colin Brewer and June Lait dismissed the political activities of radical social workers as unprofessional and charged that there was no evidence that psychodynamic social work did any good. Their belief that the professionalisation of social work around psychodynamic casework had been a sham was not so different from the argument put forward by Barbara Wootton some 20 years earlier. But, whereas left-wing opinion had been somewhat divided over Wootton's attack, much of it supporting the professionalisation of social work while question-

ing its focus on technique, Brewer and Lait's attack gained in power
from its close association with New Right ideas.

Brewer and Lait could see very little point in the vast majority of
therapeutic activities and wanted, as Wootton had done, social workers
to concentrate more on coordinating work, remedying the shortcomings of other services and referring clients to existing services. It was
perfectly appropriate, they felt, for social work to be subservient to
medicine, as it had been the pre-Seebohm local authority departments.
The idea that people did not necessarily want help with their relationships fed into the libertarian strand of New Right philosophy (King,
1987), but exhibited the same impossible desire as Wootton to take the
moral dilemmas out of social work. Brewer and Lait reserved special
criticism for the work of the FWA, deploring the number of its social
workers who were in therapy themselves and suggesting that the sort of
casework they did had no place in the public sector. In fact, the FWA
had started a fee-paying service in one area in 1971, but proceeded
slowly in developing it, there being considerable uneasiness about a
two-tier service.[40] The fee-paying service had 27 people working for it
by the end of 1979.[41] Some members of the FWA bewailed the fact that
British personal social services reached only the 'have nots', and would
have preferred the American model, whereby a sliding scale of charges
were levied,[42] but the Association remained committed to working with
the poor. It was always difficult to see how casework would relate to
the British social services. It was not possible to make casework universally available, but nor was it entirely clear what kind of clients
would benefit most from it.

In 1980, the National Institute of Social Work set up a working party
(under the chairmanship of Peter Barclay) at the request of the secretary of state to look into the role and tasks of social workers. The report
suggested a dual role for social workers, as 'counsellors' and as 'social
planners', arranging the 'social care networks' for clients in their communities (NISW, 1982). The FWA mounted a strong defence of casework in the evidence it gave to the Barclay working party. It asserted
that local authority social workers had lost touch with their 'primary
purpose'.[43] It referred to the social worker's special skills in listening
and counselling, defended the discovery and use of self in social work,
and rejected the idea of the social worker as a 'resource mobiliser'. In
his dissenting view published as an appendix to the Barclay Report,
Professor R.A. Pinker recognised the significance to social work as a
profession of moving away from the idea of casework, which, unlike

counselling, had taken account of both the personal and social aspects of human problems. The basic skills of care planning, he suggested, were employed by all personal social services professions. The recommendations of the Barclay Report thus threatened to dilute the content of social work and Pinker proved prescient in his warning that the distinction between the two grades of social work qualification, the Certificate in Social Service and the Certificate of Qualification in Social Work, would be eroded. However, in retrospect, it is possible to see how difficult it was to hold on to casework, which had become defined as the core of social work practice in the post-war period. During the 1970s, voluntary sector organisations like the FWA could assert that they were the keepers of pure social work practice. But during the 1980s, this became considerably more difficult to do. Not only was the FWA also affected by the chill winds of criticism of casework, but it additionally experienced increasing pressure to change the way in which it operated as a voluntary organisation.

At the end of the 1970s, alternative models of welfare involving a reduced role for what were dubbed at best unresponsive and at worst self-serving state bureaucracies, and a larger one for the voluntary sector were being canvassed by the political right and left (Brenton, 1985; Taylor, 1992; and Waine, 1992, provide overviews). Gladstone (1979) argued for a 'preference-guided society' where government would retain a major responsibility for financing welfare and thus secure equity, but the voluntary sector would take over much of the service delivery. The 'welfare pluralists' argued that greater participation by voluntary organisations in the delivery of social services would also mean the possibility of greater choice for users and representation of a wider spectrum of interests. For these writers, participative, decentralised pluralism was closely allied to ideas about empowerment and the importance of local democracy. In their vision of welfare provision, the voluntary sector became integral rather than remaining a supplementary or complementary partner. Professor Roger Hadley, one of the proponents of welfare pluralism (Hadley and Hatch, 1981), also sat on the Barclay working party and dissented from the report, seeking to move social work further down the road of neighbourhood-based support to informal caring networks. His idea of social work, partially adopted in the main report, was thus driven by a broader set of views about the necessity for reform of a centralised and unresponsive welfare state.

On the right, successive Conservative governments expressed their commitment to the trinity of the market, the voluntary sector and the family (Wicks, 1984) and their determination to limit the activities of the state. The main point of difference between Conservative doctrine and the welfare pluralists lay in their motivation: the Conservatives were concerned above all with economy and efficiency, the welfare pluralists with participation. And whereas the welfare pluralists favoured a slow transition to a devolved, differentiated and participative system of service delivery, the Conservatives wanted to see as rapid a transition as possible. There were nevertheless significant points of agreement, in terms of both the common desire to elevate the needs of the consumer above the professionals and the faith in capacity of the voluntary sector to expand and deliver. Government policy of course proved decisive for the fortunes of the voluntary sector, but the fact that there was substantial support for an enlarged role for voluntary organisations linked to a very different view of welfare provision from that of the Conservative Party was important and goes some way to explaining the enthusiasm with which many voluntary organisations responded to the invitation to expand.

Between 1976 and 1988, the total net income of registered charities doubled (owing in large measure to the reduction of inflation in the second half of the period). Local authority financial support for voluntary bodies rose during the first part of the 1980s (growing by 19 per cent in real terms between 1983 and 1984), but fell sharply at the end of the decade (Knapp and Saxon-Harrold, 1989; Taylor, 1992). Government sought to give a boost to charitable income through payroll giving (introduced in 1987), increased tax relief on covenants (although the reduction in the rate of direct taxes operated to reduce the income of charities from this source) and an increase in the exemption limits for charitable bequests under capital transfer tax. In fact income from donations, gifts, legacies and covenants remained fairly static throughout the decade. A major source of central government funding for the voluntary sector throughout the 1980s was the Manpower Services Commission (Addy and Scott, 1988). By the time of its demise in 1988, the MSC was providing 20 per cent of the total public sector finance to voluntary organisations, 72 per cent of which was delivered via the Community Programme, which provided temporary employment for up to one year for the long-term unemployed. Government finance via the Community Programme thus pushed voluntary organisations into expanding the number of their employees; staffing had increased by 61 per cent in the period 1976–87 in the 20 national charities investigated by Kramer *et al.* (1993) in 1989. Government thus clearly dictated the terms on which voluntary organisations were to play a greater role in service provision.

The experience of the FWA was in large measure dictated by these external financial factors. The Association had never been very successful in attracting charitable giving and its capacity to attract voluntary contributions failed to keep pace with expenditure. The Association sought new projects that were fully funded by local authorities and was conspicuously successful in being able to set up four new areas, including Milton Keynes and Northampton, but the London boroughs never provided more than two-thirds of the money needed by the London areas for their social work services and the funding gap continued to grow. In 1980, the Association gave serious consideration to the idea of promoting the use of volunteers in its area offices, something that had not happened in the post-war period.[44] The FWA also expanded on a number of other fronts. The Education Grants Advisory Service returned to the FWA umbrella and the Association expanded the non-casework side of its activities as well, taking over the administration of more trusts and almshouses. But the bulk of expansion was funded by money from the Community Programme, which meant that FWA found itself with several projects relatively unrelated to its main objectives, for example a furniture restoration scheme. When the Community Programme suddenly finished, the FWA, like many voluntary organisations, was left with considerable liabilities in terms of capital investments. This debt was in large measure responsible for the financial crisis of the organisation at the end of the decade.

The FWA's policy of expansion and diversification during the 1980s stood in sharp contrast to the tendency of the Association in previous decades to remain tightly focused and to shed activities additional to its main objects. Expansion seemed to be the order of the day, in terms of both the financial inducements and the more general political climate in which the 'entrepreneurial culture' was lauded. The FWA's director, Bob Morley, was in any case committed to diversifying FWA's activities. He wanted to broaden the remit of casework, not so as to include the coordinating, social planning activities recommended by the Barclay Report, but rather to make casework more accessible and less 'precious'. The Social Work Committee, set up to advise on the development of casework (although its terms of reference were very unclear) was abandoned – not without opposition – in 1980. Morley was also concerned to make poverty a concern of the Association again and consciously reworked the older ideas of the COS in doing this. He suggested that the COS had always stressed the importance of self-help and independence, and the importance of avoiding methods of helping that would undermine the individual's capacity to be self-maintaining. However, in late twentieth-century society it was clear that self-dependence could not be easily divorced from collective effort and it was important to campaign for the opportunities to work, learn and enjoy good health.[45] During the late 1980s, the FWA was forceful in using its statistics to show the increase in demand on its trust funds.

Given Morley's commitment to diversifying the Association's activities, he was eager to grasp any funding opportunity that came the Association's way. However, this involved significant expansion and in the process the profile of the organisation also changed considerably. Early on he exhibited a certain impatience with the power wielded by the Council under the 1972 constitution, and some members of Council got the impression that he felt that it would be better if it confined its attention to financial and administrative matters.[46] But the FWA was unfortunately particularly vulnerable to the kind of expansion that took place. The FWA's annual reports made the agency look rich, but the substantial trust funds referred to did not belong to the organisation and were only managed by it. As early as 1980, it had only three months' financial reserves.[47] It was an organisation dependent on paid labour and it relied on government for 80 per cent of its funding. By the end of the 1980s, it was saddled with an operating deficit, discovered to amount to £1 500 000 in 1990, and a very top-heavy management structure. As the organisation had expanded, so had the number of directors in charge of areas and departments; no fewer than 17 people enjoyed such a title at the end of the decade. The plans for fund raising became equally ambitious and ended in conspicuous disaster.

As a result of his study of 20 national voluntary organisations in 1989 (published in 1993), Ralph Kramer concluded that it was possible to observe a series of changes in their character, although he stressed that these were trends rather than precise descriptions. During the 1970s, the organisations could be classed as charities, providing specialised, complementary services. During the 1980s, they became more 'corporate', bigger in size, employing more staff, with more bureaucratic and formalised procedures, and providing more supplementary and alternative services. Many elements of the FWA's experience fit this pattern. What is striking, though, is the difficulty the organisation experienced in managing the change. The financial situation was not wholly within its control, given the way in which central government conducted its funding policies. But administratively the organisation was ill-equipped to handle the expansion or to monitor the financial situation. Directors were 'added-on' and patterns of communication and accountability were unclear. One respondent described meetings of the management group as being akin to a T-group, with half an hour of silence followed by 'bursting' and analysis, and then a brief run-through of the areas of work.

On the basis of a sample survey, Butler and Wilson (1990) suggested that voluntary organisations were experiencing considerable difficulties in responding to the pace of change. The FWA was in crisis, again, at the end of the 1980s and poorly placed to deal with yet another up-heaval in statutory/voluntary relationships, arguably the most significant in recent times, as government promoted the idea of managed competition and voluntary organisations were increasingly invited by local authorities to contract to provide services.

## NOTES

1. Hall (1976, p. xii, n.1) believes the term to have been coined for the Seebohm Committee, but its closeness to the much older concept of 'personal service' is apparent.
2. See above, pp. 115–16.
3. R. Huws Jones to Younghusband, 14 June 1965, Younghusband Papers, G.11/3, National Institute of Social Work.
4. Baroness Serota, 'Family Health and Social Services in the 1970s', 4th Eileen Younghusband Lecture, Younghusband Papers, G 1/11.
5. Commentators have argued endlessly over how to interpret the Committee's view of genericism. Pinker (1990) believes that it intended teams of specialised social workers; Challis and Ferlie (1987) veer towards my interpretation of paragraph 18 as the real intent; and Hall (1976) towards my interpretation of paragraph 516.
6. R.M. Titmuss, 'Social Work in the Changing World of Today', 1961, TS, Titmuss Papers, Box 104, BLPES, LSE.
7. Eileen Younghusband, 'Voluntary Organisations: Growth or Decline?', Address to the AGM of FWA's Area IV, 13 February 1973, document supplied by Helen and Roger Martyn, who were both members of Council during the 1970s (hereafter, Martyn Papers).
8. Minutes of the AGM, 21 November 1968, f. 88, FWA Archives, Dalston.
9. Memo by the FWA to the Committee on Local Authority and Allied Personal Social Services, August, 1966, A/FWA/C/C18/5, FWA Papers, Greater London Record Office.
10. This was confirmed by the Christian Organisations Research and Advisory Trust's *Survey of the Organisation and Administration of the FWA* (1970), FWA Archives, Dalston.
11. Report to Members, 31 March 1971, document supplied by Mr P. Purton, who held the offices of honorary treasurer and chairman during the 1970s and 1980s (hereafter Purton Papers).

12. Younghusband, 'Voluntary Organisations: Growth or Decline?'
13. Minutes of an EGM, 21 April 1971, f. 106, FWA Archives, Dalston.
14. Miss Lacey's Report to the Executive Committee, 11 September 1969, document supplied by Miss Rose Mary Braithwaite, Council member in the 1970s and 1980s (hereafter Braithwaite Papers); Minutes of the Board of Management, 22 July 1970, ff. 7–14, FWA, Dalston Archives.
15. Patrick Casement to Helen Martyn, reporting on a meeting of principal caseworkers, 11 July 1972, Martyn Papers.
16. Minutes of the Casework Advisory Committee, 14 October 1969, Braithwaite Papers.
17. Minutes of the Board of Management, 19 January 1971, Director's Notes on the Finance Sub-Committee, 11 January 1971, f. 70, FWA, Dalston Archives.
18. Pat Thomas, 'Intake interview', February 1970, Braithwaite Papers.
19. Lacey's Report to the Executive Committee, 11 September 1969.
20. Lacey to Thomas, 11 June 1970, Braithwaite Papers.
21. CORAT, *Survey of the Organisation and Administration of the FWA*, 1970, FWA Archives, Dalston.
22. Mrs V. Kelly to Janet Lacey, 19 January 1971, Braithwaite Papers.
23. Pat Thomas, Draft Paper, 30 April 1970, Braithwaite Papers.
24. Minutes of an Area 2 Committee Meeting, 9 June 1970, Braithwaite Papers; and Minutes of Extraordinary General Meeting, 14 July 1970, FWA Archives, Dalston.
25. Minutes of the Extraordinary General Meeting, 7 December 1971, f. 117, FWA Archives, Dalston.
26. Minutes of the Board of Management, 10 September 1970, f. 18, FWA Archives, Dalston.
27. Minutes of the Board of Management, 14 July 1970, f. 172, FWA Archives, Dalston.
28. *Report of the Study Group*, n.d., Martyn Papers.
29. Note of a Discussion with Brian Mitchell, 24 November 1972, Martyn Papers.
30. 'Director's Proposal', October 1975, Martyn Papers.
31. Minutes of the Annual General Meeting for 1977, 18 January 1978, f. 173, FWA Archives, Dalston.
32. Notes of a meeting of the study group, 19 November 1971, Martyn Papers.
33. Helen Martyn, Address to the AGM of Area 5, 20 March 1973, Martyn Papers.
34. Association Minute Book, 14 November 1990, f. 248 (Morley's reflections on the principles underlying the development plans he produced for the FWA during his term of office).
35. Brian Mitchell, 'Methods of Intervention', 1975, Martyn Papers.
36. A.A. Clark, 'Some Thoughts on Coming to FWA from a Statutory Setting', in FWA, *A Collection of Papers by Members of the Social Work Staff*, 1969, TS, FWA Archives, Dalston.
37. P.J. Casement (Principal, Area 4), 'Comment on Casework', n.d., Martyn Papers.
38. Eileen Younghusband, 'The Future of Social Work', talk given to the Child Guidance Special Interest Group, 1973, Younghusband Papers, G34.
39. Pat Thomas, personal communication, 8 September 1993.
40. 'Private Counselling Service', n.d., Martyn Papers.
41. *Annual Report of the Private Counselling Service,* 1979, Braithwaite Papers.
42. Elspeth Weldon, 'The Gap between Social Casework and Private Psychotherapy', in FWA, *A Collection of Papers by Members of the Social Work Staff*, 1969, TS, FWA Archives, Dalston.
43. FWA Evidence to the Working Party on the Role and Tasks of Social Workers, 13 April 1981, Barclay Papers, document 128, National Institute of Social Work Archives.

44. *Report* of the Working Party on a New Model for FWA Area Offices, 1980, Martyn Papers.
45. R.E. Morley, 'What Values do we stand for in relation to Social Policy and Social Benefits?', Talk for a Study Day on the Principles and Philosophy of the FWA, 21 May 1980, Braithwaite papers.
46. Fragment of a letter from Roger Martyn to Bob Morley, n.d.; and Minutes of the Organisation Committee, 15 April 1980, Martyn Papers.
47. Peter Purton's Report as Honorary Treasurer to the Annual General Meeting of the FWA, 18 November 1981, Purton Papers.

# 7. The 1990s contracts culture: not-for-profit versus charity?

The FWA has faced profound financial crisis and restructuring during the 1990s. In an effort to address its operating deficit, its new chief executive, Lynne Berry, took the decision to close half of its projects and shed one-quarter of its staff. This was happening at the same time as the government introduced its community care reforms which promised to introduce significant changes in the delivery of social services premised on the idea of making local authorities 'enablers' and increasing the role played by the voluntary and private sectors in provision. These reforms did not cause the crisis in the FWA, but they have helped shape the response taken by the organisation by setting up new parameters within which it must work.

In many respects the crisis faced by the organisation in the early 1970s contained the same main elements: financial crisis and a division of goals and purposes. Many academics have sought to explain the changes in voluntary organisations in relation to a life-cycle model, which is used to identify organisations at distinct stages in an evolutionary process associated with their age of formation (for example, Quinn and Cameron, 1983; Hasenfeld and Schmidt, 1989). There are some differences between writers as to whether organisations must pass through decline and death. In the case of the FWA, its problems have been evident for some considerable time, but it is difficult to decide whether this represents 'decline'. David Billis (1993a) has taken issue with the determinist nature of life-cycle models. Certainly, few voluntary organisations, which after all tend to attract a committed workforce, are prepared to be passive participants in a cycle of growth and decay and it is additionally remarkably difficult to fit characteristics of a particular organisation to a particular stage in the model. It may be more realistic to focus on the way in which voluntary organisations actively seek new survival strategies, a process that requires both a reinterpretation of goals and administrative acumen (see, for example, Sherrington, 1985), although it may be difficult for the members of a voluntary agency successfully to identify weakness and to achieve change. This approach seems to provide a better fit with the experience of the FWA.

The COS had come into existence with a firm theory about the social purpose of charity and the treatment of poverty, which determined its views about the nature of the relationship between the voluntary organisations and the state. The parts of the organisation – personal social work by volunteers and the raising of relief funds – were integral to its purpose. But as views about the treatment of poverty and the role of the state underwent fundamental change, so the COS ceased to be influential in social policy making and the rationale for the nature of its work disappeared. During the inter-war years, the organisation began to see casework as an end in itself, rather than as the means of securing social change. With the Beveridge Report and the post-war welfare reforms the organisation rapidly established itself as a professional casework agency, in which the social work department had little connection with the other main departments dealing with trusts, pensions, almshouses, publications, inquiries and the Citizens' Advice Bureaux. While the FWA made a successful transition from a charity dependent primarily on volunteers to a professional agency in terms of the prestige it commanded for its social work practice, two problems remained. First, it proved difficult to persuade both public and local government to support casework financially; and second, the organisation remained divided, with little communication between caseworkers and the rest and no unity of purpose. The upheaval of the early 1970s did nothing to resolve these issues, while the diversification strategies of the 1980s succeeded in masking them until the new sources of finance were suddenly withdrawn. At each crisis point in the post-war period it is thus necessary to take account of the organisation's history in order to understand its current circumstances and the way in which it responded to external factors.

In a sense, government's move at the beginning of the 1990s to give new shape to its determination to change the balance in the mixed economy of welfare such that the voluntary and private sectors played a greater part held out some promise for the FWA. The organisation was largely reliant on grant aid from local government, but this money had never covered the whole cost of providing the social work service. The idea of local authorities looking for agencies in the 'independent sector' to provide services under contract seemed to hold out the possibility of full funding. However, the FWA had to offer services that the local authority wanted to buy. While the FWA was well placed as a voluntary organisation relying largely on paid professional labour to enter contractual relationships, contracting raised difficult questions about the purpose and goals of the organisation.

## THE RESPONSE TO CRISIS

Between 1991 and 1993, the extent of the FWA's debt burden and current deficit gradually unfolded. The response of the new director, Lynne Berry, was to cut both projects that were not fully funded and a tier of management. Some of the projects were successfully floated off. Thus, in one area, a social worker attached to a GP's surgery was taken on by the GP. The main casualty was counselling services, for which it proved hard to get full funding, whether under grant or contract. The organisation began to run more services for the mentally ill under contract to health authorities. Local authorities also funded services with this client group, which alongside families and children became the FWA's most important focus of activity. Administratively, a tier of senior managers disappeared and the departments were reorganised. Social work and social work training was renamed 'families and community care', signalling the FWA's new determination to offer services that statutory authorities could easily identify and want to buy.

This degree of change proved difficult to manage. In common with many voluntary organisations in the late 1980s and 1990s, the FWA looked to a management consultancy company for help at the end of 1991. *The Economist* (1988) termed management consultants the 'new witchdoctors' of the enterprise culture. Certainly, there is a strong possibility of a clash in cultures and values between participative, democratic voluntary organisations and consultants who seek to impose clear management structures derived from the more bureaucratic worlds of the public and private sectors, and simple goals that ride roughshod over particular interests and sensibilities. The FWA accepted the financial analysis offered by the consultants, but chose not to follow their main recommendation regarding the goals of the organisation. Not surprisingly, the consultants recommended that the FWA abandon its dual purpose and put an end to the outstanding problem of division between its social work, not-for-profit service side and its more charitable endeavours. However, the identity of the Association would have been irretrievably changed by such a move. In addition, in a climate of extreme uncertainty both internally, in terms of the organisation's financial position, and externally, in terms of the question of voluntary/ statutory relations more generally, keeping options open was a strategy not without merit. Also, given the increasing level of demand on the FWA's trust funds after the changes to the social security legislation in 1986, members of the organisation were reluctant to abandon this aspect of the organisation's activities. So the FWA once again opted to remain a hybrid organisation at least until its underlying financial problems were solved, a position that remains under review as relationships between the statutory and voluntary sectors change rapidly.

## CONTRACTING

The idea of local authorities contracting with voluntary organisations to provide human services was not born with the NHS and Community Care Act of 1990. The FWA's arrangements with Milton Keynes were governed by a contract during the 1980s, and it also contracted with health authorities to provide residential care for the mentally ill early in the 1980s. However, contracting has acquired a deeper significance because of the way in which it relates to the broader aims of the community care reforms, and because it is now part and parcel of a policy to reduce statutory and increase independent provision.

Broadly speaking, the new community care policy aimed to move from service-led provision to needs-led provision, from institutional care to domiciliary care, from NHS provision to local authority provision, and from public provision to independent sector provision (Wistow *et al.*, 1994). The official guidance stated that the process of assessing need and purchasing or commissioning services, on the one hand, should be separated from the provision of services, on the other hand, in order to ensure that the needs of clients rather than the interests of providers determine the pattern of services. The idea of separating the purchase from the provision of care also linked up to government's aim of turning local authority social services departments into enablers who purchase more than they provide and so promote a mixed economy of care, which in turn has been seen as central to achieving user choice and services that are both high-quality and cost-effective (DH, 1990; DH and SSI, 1991; DH, SSI and SOSWSG, 1991). The idea of separating finance from provision has been labelled 'a quasi-market' in academic research. Le Grand (1991, 1993) has described the introduction of quasi-markets in social services as a response, first, to critics from the political right, who charged that welfare bureaucracies were wasting resources on excessive administration and protecting their own interests at the expense of those of users, and, second, to those concerned with equity as well as with efficiency. The latter set of arguments suggested that the welfare system was particularly unresponsive to the needs and wants of the very people it was set up primarily to help, the poor and disadvantaged. Quasi-markets are different from markets on both the supply and demand sides. The supplier is not necessarily out to maximise profits, nor is the ownership structure necessarily clear. On the demand side, consumer purchasing power is not expressed in cash (purchasing is not financed by the consumer, but by taxes), nor is it the consumer who exercises the choice in purchasing.

There are significant implications for voluntary organisations in the implementation of a 'purchaser/provider split' in social care as well as in the process of contracting that follows from it. Social services departments have been asked to establish the level of need and then to decide how much of what kind of service is required in consultation with other statutory authorities, voluntary organisations, users and carers. This effectively means that what voluntary organisations can offer enters a broader purchasing strategy. Conversely, a voluntary organisation must offer something that the purchaser (usually the local authority or the health authority) wishes to buy. In the past, voluntary organisations were supported by grant aid. Many still are, although the National Council for Voluntary Organisations' local authority funding survey showed that voluntary organisations lost £12m in grants during 1992–3, while contract fees increased by £78.4m (134 per cent) (*NCVO News*, 1993). Grants were never unconditional, but the profiles of many organisations were mixed in terms of service provision, information and advice activities and campaigning. Grants often supported all these and core administrative work. Under the new approach to needs-led service provision, statutory authorities are moving towards a position where they decide which services they require and then contract for them. They are no longer seeking to supplement or complement their own in-house services. For many voluntary organisations this may mean a narrowing of their activities, because the statutory authority is unlikely to want to contract for campaigning activities and is not necessarily willing to fund core administrative work.

The new culture also means a substantial change in the relationship between local authorities and voluntary organisations. Historically, voluntary organisations have taken considerable pride in their innovative work, initiating a service which may then be taken over by the local authority. State provision developed in many areas as a means of 'filling the gaps' left by the voluntary sector. However, as Saxon-Harrold (1990) has described in a study of recent trends in respect of voluntary organisations dealing with mental health and elderly people, this relationship has been reversed, with the voluntary sector being asked to fill the gaps left by the withdrawal of state provision. In other words, the dominant trend is for complementarity to mean provision 'instead of' rather than 'in addition to' the local authority. From the point of view of voluntary organisations, the message they have received in the early 1990s has been mixed. The statutory authorities that are supposed to be enabling them to do more in terms of service provision have also (especially in inner London) cut financial aid to the tune of 20–25 per cent. Voluntary agencies also have reason to be wary of the power imbalance involved in working the new relationship. If they are asked to provide a particular service, can they refuse? Soon after the passing of the 1990 Act, Hoyes and Means (1991) reported some agencies feeling that they had little choice but to agree to provide what the statutory authority wanted.

The draft guidance on the community care legislation issued in 1990 suggested a firm functional split between purchaser and provider functions for social services departments along the lines of changes taking place in health authorities and thus also implied a market relationship between the statutory authority and any possible voluntary organisation provider. Such an approach is not without irony, given the economists' theories of the voluntary sector as the product of market failure and lack of trust.[1] Both local authorities and the voluntary sector reacted strongly against this idea. The Association of Metropolitan Authorities (1990) acknowledged that all the factors linking local authorities and voluntary organisations 'will require a rethink' but insisted that local authorities should avoid making a rigid purchaser/provider split, seeking instead 'to achieve a redefined form of partnership' (p. 9). The National Council for Voluntary Organisations (1990) also deplored any move towards contracting on the basis of price-based competition: 'A critical question in this debate is "who does what best?" The concept of partnership needs to be preserved, even if the award of a particular contract has to be made with due regard to financial proprieties' (para. 2.12).

The revised 1991 guidance, and in particular the Price Waterhouse document (DH and Price Waterhouse, 1991) on purchaser/provider roles within SSDs, substantially modified the earlier impression of a model imported from the private sector. The document acknowledged the importance of trust and stated that one of the chief strengths of the relationship between the statutory and voluntary sectors was the closeness of contact with in-house and community providers and concluded that the new relationship was best conceived of as 'being a contract culture involving close ongoing relationships with providers, rather than being based upon anonymous short term price competition' (p. 11). Nevertheless, as Common and Flynn (1992) remarked, collaboration between purchaser, provider, service user and carer 'does not fit closely with the market definitions of buying and selling'.

The literature relating to the likely impact of these changes on voluntary organisations is overwhelmingly American, because the USA has some 20 years' experience in contracting for human services. The major issues raised by the US literature for the voluntary sector are the effect of contracting on the autonomy and independence of voluntary organisations; possible gains in terms of increased security of funding and greater clarity of role; and the effects on the internal management of organisations (de Hoog, 1984; Kettner and Martin, 1987; Demone and Gibelman, 1988; Kramer and Terrell, 1984; Kramer, 1990). The conclusions tend to be more positive about the capacity of organisations to preserve their independence than anything else. Kramer in particular has suggested that traditional partnership relationships in which voluntary organisations usually rely on grant aid actually tend to minimise the power of the voluntary agency, which is cast in the role of supplicant rather than partner, and that contracts offer the best way for a voluntary organisation to balance its need for independence against government's need for accountability. However, considerable caution has to be used in applying these conclusions, given the very different context in the USA: statutory services were never providers on the same scale in that country; the pattern of funding of American voluntary organisations has been rather different, with agencies relying on funds from a multiplicity of government organisations and on non-governmental sources for core activities, development and advocacy; and the shift to contracts has been very different. Whereas the USA 'drifted' into a contracts culture, in Britain the change has been dictated by government policy.

The British literature is as yet sparse and tends to be more equivocal. In a study of contracts within one voluntary organisation, Crossroads, Hedley and Rochester (1991) found only 15 per cent of the local organisations to be operating under contract. While there was evidence that negotiations preceding the contract had usually been protracted, Hedley and Rochester concluded that the problems of growth and formalisation that they observed in the organisations would 'have arisen independently of the development of contracting arrangements' (para 13.6). They conceded that the organisations might be in something of a 'honeymoon', transitional period regarding contracts (most services under contract were still complementary) but they were on the whole optimistic that voluntary organisations would remain favoured providers.

The Volunteer Centre (Hedley and Rochester, 1993) contacted 500 organisations in May 1993. They received 190 replies, out of which 37 per cent were running contracts. Of these, 40 per cent said that contracts were an improvement and only 10 per cent said that they considered their organisations to be worse off. In their more detailed study of 12 contracts, Common and Flynn (1992) emphasised the importance of trust and condemned adversarial contractual relationships. They found that, while relationships between voluntary agencies and statutory authorities became more formal during the period of negotiation, they tended to relax afterwards, although there was variation in the degree of formality with which the contract was managed. Running a contract is significantly different from administering a grant; one American commentator has referred to relationships around the contract taking on a life of their own (Gronbjerg, 1991). The process of formalisation may encourage greater clarity, but also serve to increase the bureaucratic aspects of the organisation, which militate against flexibility and responsiveness, just as competition tends to militate against trust (Lewis, 1993, 1994).

Contracts do not yet dominate voluntary/statutory relationships, but the six key tasks set out by the NHS Management Executive and the Social Services Inspectorate for 1993–4 referred both to the need to begin to shift the balance of resources towards non-residential care and to the development of joint commissioning with health authorities (EL (93) 18/CI (93) 12). In fact, while in 1992 Knapp *et al.* reported that only three of the 24 local authorities they looked at were enthusiastic about enabling, since the beginning of 1993 SSDs have shown considerably more interest in commissioning strategies. The grant-aid culture is disappearing and with it the 'special relationship' between the statutory and the voluntary sector. Voluntary agencies may still be preferred as providers, not least because of the considerable quantities of volunteer labour that many can deliver, but local authorities are increasingly talking about the importance of securing 'level playing-fields' for independent providers of all kinds and for their own in-house providers.

The impact of the contract culture on the FWA has been marked in terms of effecting a change in culture, even though income from contracts actually fell between 1991 and 1993. The organisation has experienced arbitrary cuts in the funding received under two separate contractual arrangements, which casts doubt on whether contracts can provide greater security for voluntary organisations. The effect on the goals of the organisation has perhaps been greatest, with local offices seeking to provide and market what statutory authorities will buy. One local authority has strictly dictated the terms of access for users, taking away from the Association all control over its client group. In addition, the responsibility falling on paid managers as opposed to voluntary trustees has become more apparent as decision making has become more complicated. While policy decisions in the organisation have long been taken by the paid staff, the decisions on restructuring the organisation in response to financial crisis and on how to redefine its activities have been large ones for paid staff to handle. However, the phenomenon of paid staff taking heavy decision-making responsibility with only minimal policy guidance from trustees has become more generally evident in voluntary organisations during the late 1980s and 1990s (Harris, 1989; Hedley and Rochester, 1992; Lewis, 1994).

The cultural shift within the FWA has been most profound for its social work staff. One described the contracting culture as being 'in a shopping mall with the lights out'. Social workers have had to become familiar with costing services and marketing them. Some areas have made strong efforts to hang on to the system of supervision and case conferences. But they have had to adjust to practice in which method is subordinated to tasks rather than vice versa, and a range of models are offered to suit both a variety of clients and statutory preferences. In a sense, the social work staff have been forced to take on both the roles advocated by the 1982 Barclay Report. They have become mediators and social planners, while endeavouring to continue to practise casework skills in a variety of settings. To some extent their experience mirrors that of social workers in SSDs, who are dealing with assessment of individual need, which may be more or less mechanistic, and who are experiencing the introduction of 'care management', which is subject to a number of different definitions, but which puts a premium on social planning and care coordination rather than counselling skills.

However, the position is considerably more complex than the mere redefinition of social work envisaged by Barclay. Because of the introduction of purchaser/provider splits, social work in the statutory sector has on the whole (although by no means entirely) become a purchasing function, whereas social work in the voluntary sector is likely to be defined in terms of providing. In the new social care market social workers must therefore negotiate both dimensions of their role, counselling and care coordination, as well as the boundary between purchasing and providing. Whereas, in the 1970s, the FWA had acted as the keeper of the casework culture, there is little chance of this happening in the current climate.

## THE FUTURE OF THE 'NEW PARTNERSHIP'

The American literature has stressed that contracts offer voluntary agencies the opportunity to become partners rather than supplicants. However, for agencies that are funded largely by government, it is difficult to see how the balance of power can ever rest with the voluntary agency. Within the new contracts culture (inside SSDs as well as between voluntary and statutory authorities), purchasers 'call the shots'. If a voluntary organisation becomes a large, monopoly provider of a hitherto mainstream local authority service, it may have considerable bargaining power, but it should be remembered that the *aim* of the reforms is to avoid replacing monopoly local authority providers with single independent providers. Furthermore, if provision of social services does become increasingly competitive, then voluntary agencies will face competition from private agencies. So far this has been limited for anything beyond residential and nursing homes.

Contracts tend to assume that the contractor is the same form of organisation as the purchaser and do not make allowance for different forms of management. Taylor and Hoggett (1993) have considered the potential for remaking contractors in the image of the purchaser. If indeed the historical role of the voluntary sector is to undergo profound change, such that it ceases to be either complementary or supplementary to the statutory sector and becomes an alternative provider, possibly of first resort, then the implications for mission, management and governance are huge. Salamon (1987) has suggested that at present the voluntary and statutory sectors are complementary in terms of their strengths and weaknesses, making collaboration sensible, but quasi-market relationships are not inherently sympathetic to a collaborative form of partnership. Indeed, there is a profound tension between the injunction to develop competition on the one hand, and the trust necessary for joint working, on the other (Hunter, 1992). The precise form the new partnership will take in the new contracts culture is hard to predict.

Billis (1993b) has warned of the dangers of an instrumental use of the voluntary sector which emphasises only those attributes that are of direct use to government. The process of contracting, which carries with it the idea of formalising arrangements between the parties and of producing a uniform, high quality service, highlights both the tensions inherent in the relationship between the statutory and voluntary sectors and the ambiguities inherent in the nature of voluntary organisations. Billis (1989) has argued that, while voluntary organisations are primarily associational, they overlap both the personal and bureaucratic worlds. The management of ambiguity requires an understanding of the ground rules of both the associational and bureaucratic worlds, an appreciation of membership, mission, informality and democracy, on the one hand, and managerial authority and accountability, levels of decision making, career progression, staff development, conditions of service and explicit policy making, on the other. Voluntary organisations balance the demands of bureaucracy and association. It may be suggested that contracting will tend to shift the balance towards the former. Certainly, Barry Knight's (1993) report on voluntary action, in which he pushed enabling to its logical conclusion and advocated dividing voluntary organisations into autonomous campaigners, on the one hand, and a 'third sector' of contracting, not-for-profit service providers, on the other, rode roughshod over the participatory and associational nature of voluntary agencies. The term 'partnership' has served to gloss the problems inherent in a relationship between a formal bureaucratic statutory organisation and one that is more ambiguous. The new basis for partnership may be firmer in so far as voluntary organisations may come to adopt more bureaucratic features, but this also implies a significant change in the nature of voluntary organisations, which may not be cost-free.

Using the FWA's experience as a prism, it looks as though the wheel has come full circle from the late nineteenth century to the late twentieth, when voluntary organisations are once more going to take the centre of the stage. However, such a comparison is too superficial. The conditions of voluntary action are very different from what they were a hundred years ago. The FWA cannot dictate the terms of its participation as the COS was able to do. That said, the financial condition of the COS was never robust in its early years and perhaps the most striking feature of the organisation has been its capacity to regroup and survive. In 1994, the agency adopted a new 'strapline': 'meeting need'. In so far as need in the late twentieth century continues to be as much for material as for emotional help, the two sides of the FWA's activities remain relevant, albeit hard to manage within a single organisation. Like so many voluntary, service-providing organisations, the FWA finds itself squeezed between the pressures exerted by the contracts culture, on the one hand, and the increasing numbers of people needing its services, on the other. Social workers within the organisation must try and balance work as managers, coordinators and caseworkers. The crisis of the 1990s has been the most severe for the FWA and its position remains fragile. In the current climate the most difficult issue for the organisation is perhaps not so much the management of change, rapid as this is, but the management of uncertainty, just as it is for an increasing number of the population at large.

## NOTE

1. See above, pp. 3–4.

# Appendix: respondents interviewed

Lynne Berry, Director, 24 May 1993.

Rose Mary Braithwaite, former Council member, 6 October 1993.

Haddy Davis, FWA Service Manager, 5 November 1993.

Malcolm Ford, former Casework Administrative Officer and Acting Director, 15 September 1993.

Professor Maurice Kogan, former Council member, 27 September 1993.

Helen Martyn, former Council member, 5 July 1993.

Roger Martyn, former Council member and Chairman, 5 July 1993.

Bob Morley, former Director, 6 June 1993.

Andrew Pidgeon, FWA Regional Practice Teacher, 18 November 1993.

Ken Smith, former FWA Principal Social Worker, 17 November 1993.

Marjorie Taylor, former Council member and Chairman, 25 August 1993.

Mike Vockins, FWA Team Leader, 4 November 1993.

# Bibliography

This bibliography contains all material, published and unpublished, that is referred to in the text and available in libraries. In the case of unpublished works, the library where the material may be found is given. Archival material and unattributed articles are referred to in the notes.

Adams, B.K. (1976) 'Charity, Voluntary Work and Professionalization in late Victorian and Edwardian England, with special reference to the COS and Guilds of Help', unpublished MA thesis, University of Sussex.

Addy, T. and Scott, D. (1988) *Fatal Impacts? The MSC and Voluntary Action*, Manchester: William Temple Foundation.

Anon. (1942) *Thomas Hancock Nunn. The Life and Work of a Social Reformer*, London: Baines and Scarsbrook.

Archbishop of Canterbury (1891) *The Science of Charity*, Occasional Paper, no. 19, London: COS.

Association of Metropolitan Authorities (1990) *Contracts for Social Care: The Local Authority View*, London: AMA.

Astbury, B.E. (1931) *A Restatement of Casework*, Occasional Paper, no. 36, London: COS.

Astbury, B.E. (1938) *Material Welfare: Report of the Third International Conference on Social Work*, London: Le Play House Press.

Astbury, B.E. (1943) 'The COS and the Future', *Social Work*, **2**, October.

Attlee, C.R. (1920) *The Social Worker*, London: G. Bell and Sons.

Bailey, R. and Brake, M. (1975) *Radical Social Work*, London: Edward Arnold.

Bailward, W.A. (1908) 'The Relation of Legal Relief to Private Charity', *Proceedings of the 36th Annual Poor Law Conference*.

Bailward, W.A. (1910) 'The Charity Organisation Society', *Quarterly Review*, **CCVI**, January.

Bailward, W.A. (1920) *The Slippery Slope and other Papers on Social Subjects*, London: John Murray.

Bamford, Terry (1990) *The Future of Social Work*, London: Macmillan.

Bannister, K. *et al.* (1955) *Social Casework in Marital Problems, The Development of the Psychodynamic Approach*, London: Tavistock.

Barnett, Henrietta (1884) 'What has the COS to do with Social Reform?', *Charity Organisation Reporter*, 19 April.

Barnett, Samuel (1895) 'Friendly Criticism of the Charity Organisation Society', *Charity Organisation Review*, August.

Barnett, Samuel and Barnett, Henrietta (1894) *Practicable Socialism*, 2nd edn, London: Longman, Green and Co.

Best, G. (1964) *Temporal Pillars*, Cambridge: Cambridge University Press.

Beveridge, William (1924) *Insurance for All and Everything*, New Way Series, no. 7, London: The Daily News Ltd.

Beveridge, W. (1948) *Voluntary Action. A Report on Methods of Social Advance*, London: Allen and Unwin.

Billis, D. (1989) *A Theory of the Voluntary Sector: Implications for Policy and Practice*, Working Paper no. 5, Centre for Voluntary Organisation, LSE.

Billis, D. (1993a) 'Organizational change and Crisis in Nonprofits', paper presented at the annual meeting of ARNOVA, Toronto.

Billis, D. (1993b) *Organising Public and Voluntary Agencies*, Routledge, London.

Blacker, C.P. (ed.) (1937) *A Social Problem Group?*, Oxford: Oxford University Press.

Blacker, C.P. (1952) *Problem Families: Five Inquiries*, London: Eugenics Society.

Board of Education and Board of Control (1927) *Report of the Mental Deficiency Committee*, London: HMSO.

Bosanquet, B. (1890) 'The Antithesis between Individualism and Socialism Philosophically Considered', *Charity Organisation Review*, September.

Bosanquet, B. (1892) 'The Limitations of the Poor Law', *The Economic Journal*, **2**, (6).

Bosanquet, B. (1893) 'The Principles and Chief Dangers of the Administration of Charity', in J. Addams (ed.), *Philanthropy and Social Progress. Seven Essays*, New York: Thomas Y. Crowell and Co.

Bosanquet, B. (1895a) 'The Duties of Citizenship', in B. Bosanquet (ed.), *Aspects of Social Reform*, London: Macmillan.

Bosanquet, B. (1895b) 'Character in its bearing of Social Causation', in B. Bosanquet (ed.), *Aspects of Social Reform*, London: Macmillan.

Bosanquet, B. (1898) 'Idealism in Social Work', *Charity Organisation Review*, March.

Bosanquet, B. (1899) *The Philosophical Theory of the State*, London: Macmillan.

Bosanquet, B. (1901) 'The Meaning of Social Work', *International Journal of Ethics*, **11**.

Bosanquet, B. (1909) 'I. The Majority Report', *Sociological Review*, **2**.

Bosanquet, B. (1910) 'Charity Organisation and the Majority', *International Journal of Ethics*, **20**.

Bosanquet, B. (1917) *Social and International Ideals. Being Studies in Patriotism*, London: Macmillan.

Bosanquet, H. (1893) 'Thorough Charity', *Charity Organisation Review*, June.

Bosanquet, H. (1896) *Rich and Poor*, London: Macmillan.

Bosanquet, H. (1897) 'The Psychology of Social Progress', *International Journal of Ethics*, **7**.

Bosanquet, H. (1898) *The Standard of Life and other Studies*, London: Macmillan.

Bosanquet, H. (1903a) *The Strength of the People. A Study in Social Economics*, London: Macmillan.

Bosanquet, H. (1903b) *The Poverty Line*, London: COS.

Bosanquet, H. (1906) *The Family*, London: Macmillan.

Bosanquet, H. (1914) *Social Work in London, 1869–1912*, London: John Murray.

Braithwaite, C. (1938) *The Voluntary Citizen: an Enquiry into the Place of Philanthropy in the Community*, London: Methuen.

Branson, N. (1974) *Poplarism 1919–35. George Lansbury and the Councillors*, London: Lawrence and Wishart.

Brasnett, Margaret (1969) *Voluntary Social Action. A History of the National Council of Social Service*, London: NCSS.

Brenton, Maria (1985) *The Voluntary Sector in British Social Services*, London: Longman.

Brewer, Colin and Lait, June (1980) *Can Social Work Survive?*, London: Temple Smith.

Briskin, Sidney J. (1958) 'Casework and Present Day Trends', *Social Work*, **15**, October.

British Association of Social Work (1977) *The Social Work Task*, London: BASW.

Brockington, C. Fraser (1949) *Problem Families*, Occasional Papers, no. 2, London: British Social Hygiene Council.

Brown, Sybil Clement (1939) 'The Methods of Social Case-Workers', in F.C. Bartlett, M. Ginsberg, E.J. Lindgren and R.H. Thouless (eds), *The Study of Society*, London: Kegan Paul, Trench and Trubner.

Brown, Sybil Clement (1945) 'Training for Social Work', *Social Work*, 3, October.

Bruno, F. (1937) 'Foreign Social Work', *Social Work Year Book, 1937*, New York: Russell Sage Foundation.

Butler, R.J. and Wilson, D.C. (1990) *Managing Voluntary and Non-profit Organisations*, London: Routledge.

Butrym, Zofia (1976) *The Nature of Social Work*, London: Macmillan.

Byles, A. Holden (1908) 'The Larger Work of the Guilds of Help', *Progress*, no. 10, April.

C. 123. (1870) *Twenty Second Annual Report of the Poor Law Board, 1869 –70*, Appendix A., no. 4.

C. 516 (1872) *First Report of the Local Government Board, 1871–2*, Appendix 20.

C. 1255 (1875) *Poor Laws in Foreign Countries. Report to the Local Government Board.*

C. 4402–1 (1885) *Report of the Royal Commission on Housing of the Working Classes*, vol. II, *Minutes of Evidence*.

C. 534 (1888) *Reports on the Elberfield Poor Law System.*

Cd 4499 (1909) *Report of the Royal Commission on the Poor Laws and the Relief of Distress.*

Cd 5664 (1911) *Report to the President of the Local Government Board on Guilds of Help in England.*

Cd 7698 (1914) *Minutes of Evidence taken by the Committee on Sickness Benefit Claims under the National Health Insurance Act.*

Cmd 4495 (1934) *Report of the Departmental Committee on Sterilization.*

Cmd 8710 (1952) *Report of the Committee on the Law and Practice Relating to Charitable Trusts.*

Cmnd 1191 (1960) *Report on Children and Young Persons.*

Cmnd 3703 (1968) *Report of the Committee on Local Authority and Allied Personal Social Services.*

Cahill, M. and Jowitt, T. (1980) 'The New Philanthropy: The Emergence of the Bradford City Guild of Help', *Journal of Social Policy*, 9, 359–82.

Challis, David and Ferlie, Ewan (1987) 'The Myth of Generic Practice: Specialisation in Social Work', *Journal of Social Policy*, 17, (1).

Chance, William (1895) *The Better Administration of the Poor Law*, London: Swan Sonnenschein.

Collini, S. (1979) *Liberalism and Sociology. L.T. Hobhouse and Political Argument in England, 1880–1914*, Cambridge: Cambridge University Press.

Collini, S. (1985) 'The Idea of "Character" in Victorian Political Thought', *Transactions of the Royal Historical Society*, **35**.

Collini, S. (1991) *Public Moralists. Political Thought and Intellectual Life in Britain, 1850–1930*, Oxford: Clarendon Press.

Collis, A. (1958) 'Casework in a Statutory and Voluntary Setting', *Social Work*, **15**, April.

Collis, A. (1961) 'Social work: A Current Assessment of Training and Related Topics', *Social Work*, **18**, July.

Common, R. and Flynn, N. (1992) *Contracting for Care*, York: Joseph Rowntree Foundation.

Cooper, Joan (1983) *The Creation of the British Personal Social Services, 1962–1974*, London: Heinemann.

Cormack, Una (1945) 'Developments in Casework', in A.F.C. Bourdillon (ed.), *Voluntary Social Services. Their Place in the Modern State*, London: Methuen.

COS (n.d., but c. 1915) *A Specimen of the Case Work of the London (England) Charity Organisation Society*, London: COS.

COS (1870) *Report of a Sub-Committee on House to House Visitation*, London: COS.

COS (1881) *Papers*, Occasional Paper, no. 6: 'Loans', London: Longmans, Green and Co.

COS (1891) *First Report of a Special Committee of the COS appointed to consider the best means of dealing with school children alleged to be in want of food*, London: COS

COS (1893) *The Better Way of Assisting School Children*, London: Swan Sonnenschein.

COS (1919) *51st Annual Report for 1918–19*, London.

COS (1920) *52nd Annual Report for 1919–20*, London.

COS (1924) *56th Annual Report for 1923–4*, London.

COS (1925) *57th Annual Report for 1924–5*, London.

COS (1934) *66th Annual Report for 1933–4*, London.

Crossman, R. (1976) 'The Role of the Volunteer in the Modern Social Services' in A.H. Halsey (ed.), *Traditions of Social Policy. Essays in Honour of Violet Butler*, Oxford: Blackwell.

Cunliffe, Muriel (1958) 'The Use of Supervision in Casework Practice', *Social Work*, **15**, January.

Cunliffe, Muriel (1960) 'Family Casework'. *Social Work*, **17**, January.

D'Aeth (1914) 'The Social Welfare Movement', *Economic Review*, **XXIV**.

D'Aeth (1915a) 'Local Representation Committees', *Charity Organisation Review*, July.

D'Aeth (1915b) War Relief Agencies and the Guild of Help Movement', *Progress* X.

Dean of Norwich (1910) *The Sphere of Voluntary Agencies under the Minority Report*, London: The National Committee to Promote the Break-up of the Poor Law.

de Hoog, R.H. (1984) *Contracting Out for Human Services*, Albany, New York: SUNY Press.

Demone, H.W. Jr. and Gibelman, M. (eds) (1988) *Services for Sale. Purchasing Health and Human Services*, New Brunswick: Rutgers University Press.

Dendy, H. (1893) 'Thorough Charity', *Charity Organisation Review*, June.

Dendy, H. (1895a) 'The Children of Working London', in B. Bosanquet (ed.), *Aspects of Social Reform*, London: Macmillan.

Dendy, H. (1895b) 'The Industrial Residuum', in B. Bosanquet (ed.), *Aspects of Social Reform*, London: Macmillan.

DH (Department of Health) (1990) *Community Care in the Next Decade and Beyond, Policy Guidance*, London: HMSO.

DH (Department of Health) and Price Waterhouse (1991) *Implementing Community Care. Purchaser, Commissioner and Provider Roles*, London: HMSO.

DH and SSI (Department of Health and Social Services Inspectorate) (1991) *Purchase of Service*, London: HMSO.

DH, SSI and SOSWSG (Department of Health, Social Services Inspectorate and Scottish Office Social Work Services Group) (1991) *Care Management and Assessment. Managers' Guide*, London: HMSO.

Digby, A. (1989) *British Welfare Policy*, London: Faber and Faber.

Donnison D.V. (1954) *The Neglected Child and the Social Services*, Manchester: Manchester University Press.

Donnison, D.V. and Chapman, V. (1975) *Social Policy and Administration. Studies in the Development of Social Services at the Local Level*, 2nd edn, London: Allen and Unwin.

Dunn-Gardner, R. (1895) *The Training of Volunteers*, COS Occasional Paper, no. 46, London: COS.

*The Economist* (1988) 'Managing Consultants', 13 February.

Ehrenreich, John H. (1985) *The Altruistic Imagination. A History of Social Work and Social Policy in the US*, Ithica: Cornell University Press.

EI (93) 18/CI (93) 12, Department of Health Letter, 'Implementing Caring for People', 15 March 1993.

Emmet, Dorothy (1962) 'Ethics and the Social Worker', *The British Journal of Psychiatric Social Work*, **6**, no. 4.

Esping Andersen, Gösta (1990) *The Three Worlds of Welfare Capitalism*, Cambridge: Polity.

Fabian Women's Group (1911) *How the National Insurance Bill affects Women*, London: FWG.

Family Welfare Association (1946) *Annual Report 1945–6*, London.

Family Welfare Association (1961) *The Family. Patients or Clients?*, London: The Faith Press.

Fido, J. (1977) 'The COS and Social Casework in London, 1869–1900', in A.P. Donajgrodski (ed.), *Social Control in Nineteenth Century Britain*, London: Croom Helm.

Finlayson, Geoffrey (1990) 'A Moving Frontier: Voluntarism and the State in British Social Welfare', *Twentieth Century British History*, **1**, (2).

Finn, Walter H. (ed.) (1973) *Family Therapy in Social Work*, Conference Papers, London: FWA.

Flexner, A. (1915) 'Is Social Work a Profession?', *Proceedings of the National Conference of Charities and Correction, 42nd. Annual Session, 1915*, Chicago.

Follett, M.P. (1918) *The New State. Group Organization: the Solution of Popular Government*, London: Longmans, Green and Co.

Fox, Enid (1993) 'District Nursing and the Work of District Nursing Associations in England and Wales, 1900–1948', unpublished PhD thesis, University of London.

Gladstone, F. (1979) *Voluntary Action in a Changing World*, London: Bedford Square Press.

Goldberg, E. Matilda and Warburton, R. William (1979) *Ends and Means in Social Work. The Development and Outcome of a Case Review System for Social Workers*, London: Allen and Unwin.

Goldberg, E. Matilda, Gibbons, J. and Sinclair, I (1985) *Problems, Tasks and Outcomes*, London: Allen and Unwin.

Grisewood, W. (1909) 'The Place of Relief in the Service of the Poor', *Second National Conference of Guilds of Help, 1909*, London.

Gronbjerg, K. (1987) 'Patterns of Institutional Relations in the Welfare State: Public Mandates and the Nonprofit Sector', *Journal of Voluntary Action Research*, **16**.

Gronbjerg, K. (1991) 'Managing Grants and Contracts: the Case of Four Nonprofit Social Service Organizations', *Nonprofit and Voluntary Sector Quarterly*, **20**.

Hadley, R. and Hatch, S. (1981) *Social Welfare and the Failure of the State: Centralised Social Services and Participatory Alternatives*, London: Allen and Unwin.

Hall, Phoebe (1976) *Reforming the Welfare. The Politics of Change in the Personal Social Services*, London: Heinemann.

Hancock-Nunn, Thomas (n.d.) *The Minority Report*, London: n.p., BLPES.

Hancock-Nunn, Thomas (1909) *A Council of Social Welfare. A Note and Memorandum on the Report of the Royal Commission on the Poor Law and Relief of Distress as to the Functions and Constitution of the new Public Assistance Authority and its Local Committees*, London: n.p.

Hancock-Nunn, Thomas (1914) 'Voluntary Workers at Newcastle', *Economic Review*, **XXIV**.

Hansmann, Henry (1987) 'Economic Theories of Non Profit Organisations', in W.W. Powell (ed.), *The Non Profit Sector. A Research Handbook*, New Haven: Yale University Press.

Harbert, W.B. (1972) 'Voluntary Body Seeks a Future', *British Hospital Journal and Social Services Review*, **15**.

Harris, Bernard (1991) 'Unemployment and Charity in the South Wales Coalfield between the Wars', paper given to the Summer School of the Institute for Contemporary British History, July.

Harris, José (1972) *Employment and Politics*, Oxford: Oxford University Press.

Harris, José (1983) 'The Transition to High Politics in English Social Policy, 1880–1914', in M. Bentley and J. Stevenson (eds) *High and Low Politics in Modern Britain*, Oxford: Clarendon Press.

Harris, José (1990) 'Society and the State in Twentieth Century Britain', in F.M.L. Thompson (ed.), *The Cambridge Social History of Britain 1750–1950*, vol. 3, *Social Agencies and Institutions*, Cambridge: Cambridge University Press.

Harris, José (1993) *Private Lives, Public Spirit. A Social History of Britain, 1870–1914*, Oxford: Oxford University Press.

Harris, M. (1989) *Management Committees in Practice: A Study in Local Voluntary Leadership*, Working Paper no. 7, Centre for Voluntary Organisation, LSE.

Harrison, B. (1982) *Peaceable Kingdom*, Oxford: Clarendon Press.

Harrison, J.L. (1910) 'Cooperation between Charity and the Poor Law; a plea for its more general application', *Proceedings of the 22nd. Annual Poor Law Conference of the North Midland Districts. 1910*, London: P.S. King.

Hartshorn, Alma E. (1982) *Milestone in Education for Social Work. The Carnegie Experiment, 1954–8*, Dunfermline: Carnegie UK Trust.

Hasenfeld, Y. and Schmidt, H. (1989) 'The Life Cycle of Human Service Organizations: An Administrative Perspective', *Administrative Leadership in the Social Services*, **13**, (3/4).

Hedley, R. and Rochester, C. (1991) *Contracts at the Crossroads*, London: Association of Crossroads Care Attendance Schemes.

Hedley, R. and Rochester, C. (1992) *Understanding Management Committees: A Look at Volunteer Management Committee Members*, Berkamstead: The Volunteer Centre.

Hedley, R. and Rochester, C. (1993) *Volunteering and the Contract Culture*, Berkamstead: The Volunteer Centre.

Henriques, J.Q. (1938) *A Citizen's Guide to Social Service*, London: Allen and Unwin.

Hill, Octavia (1869) 'Organised Work among the Poor. Suggestions founded on four years' management of a London court', *Macmillans*, **20**.

Hill, Octavia (1872) 'The Work of Volunteers in the Organisation of Charity', *Macmillans*, **24**.

Hill, Octavia (1874) 'The Elberfield System in London', *Charity Organisation Reporter*, 317–21.

Hill, Octavia (1875) *Homes of the London Poor*, London: Macmillan.

Hill, Octavia (1877a) *District Visiting*, London: COS.

Hill, Octavia (1877b) *Our Common Land*, London: Macmillan.

Hill, Octavia (1889) *The Charity Organisation Society*, Occasional Paper, no. 15, London: COS.

Hill, Octavia (1898) 'The Need of Thoroughness in Charitable Work', *Charity Organisation Review*, November

Himmelfarb, G. (1986) *Marriage and Morals among the Victorians*, London: Faber and Faber.

Hodson, A.L. (1909) *Letters from a Settlement*, London: Edward Arnold.

Hong, Young Sun (1989) 'The Politics of Welfare Reform and the Dynamics of the Public Sphere: Church, Society, and the State in the Making of the Social-Welfare System in Germany, 1830–1930', unpublished PhD diss., University of Michigan.

Howarth, E. (1951) 'The Present Dilemma of Social Casework', *Social Work*, **8**, April.

Howe, David (1987) *An Introduction to Social Work Theory*, London: Wildwood House.

Hoyes, L. and Le Grand, J. (1991) *Markets in Social Care Services*, Bristol: School for Advanced Urban Studies.

Hoyes, L. and Means, R. (1991) *Implementing the White Paper on Community Care*, DQM Paper no. 4, Bristol: School for Advanced Urban Studies.

Humphreys, Robert (1991) 'The Poor Law and Charity. The COS in the Provinces, 1870–1890', unpublished PhD thesis, University of London.

Hunter, D.J. (1992) 'To Market! To Market! A New Dawn for Community Care?', *Health and Social Care*, **1**.

Irvine, Elizabeth (1954) 'Research into Problem Families: Theoretical Questions arising from Dr. Blacker's Investigations', *British Journal of Psychiatric Social Work*, no. 9, May.

Iselin, the Rev. Henry (1912) 'The Story of a Children's Care Committee', *Economic Review*, **22**, January.

Jennings, Hilda (1930) *The Private Citizen in Public Social Work. An Account of the Voluntary Child Care Committee System in London*, London: Allen and Unwin.

Jones, David Caradog (ed.) (1934) *The Social Survey of Merseyside*, vol. 3, Liverpool: Liverpool University Press and Hodder and Stoughton.

Jones, Kathleen (1984) *Eileen Younghusband. A Biography*, Occasional Papers in Social Administration, no. 76, London: Bedford Square Press.

Kanthack, Emelia (1907) *The Preservation of Infant Life*, London: H.K. Lewis.

Keeling, Dorothy C. (1961) *The Crowded Stairs*, London: National Council of Social Service.

Keenleyside, Mary (1958) 'Development in Casework Methods', *Social Work*, **15**, October.

Keith-Lucas, Alan (1953) 'The Political Theory Implicit in Social Casework Theory', *American Political Science Review*, **XLVII**, (4).

Kettner, Peter M. and Martin, L.L. (1987) *Purchase of Service Contracting*, Newbury Park, Calif.: Sage.

Kidd, Alan J. (1984) 'Charity Organization and the Unemployed in Manchester, c. 1870–1914', *Social History*, **9**.

King, D. (1987) *The New Right. Politics, Markets and Citizenship*, Basingstoke: Macmillan.

Kirkman-Gray, B. and Hutchins, B. L. (eds) (1908) *Philanthropy and the State, or Social Politics*, London: P.S. King.

Knapp, Martin and Saxon-Harrold, Susan (1989) *The British Voluntary Sector*, Discussion Paper 645, PSSRU, University of Kent.

Knapp, Martin *et al.* (1992) 'From Providing to Enabling: Local Authorities and the Mixed Economy of Care', *Public Administration*, **70**.

Knight, Barry (1993) *Voluntary Action*, London: HMSO.

Kramer, R.M. (1990) 'Non-profit Organizations and the Welfare State', in H.K. Anheier and W. Seibel (eds) *The Third Sector. Comparative Studies of Non-Profit Organizations*, New York: de Guyter.

Kramer, R.M. and Terrell, P. (1984) 'Contracting for Social Services: Process Management and Resource Dependencies', *Social Service Review*, **61**, (1).

Kramer, R.M., Lorentzen, H., Melief, W.B. and Pasquinelli, S. (1993) *Privatization in Four European Countries. Comparative Studies in Government–Third Sector Relationships*, Armonk, New York: M.E. Sharpe.

Kuhnle, S. and Selle, P. (1992) 'Government and Voluntary Organisations – A Relational Perspective', in S. Kuhnle and P. Selle (eds) *Government and Voluntary Organisations*, Aldershot: Avebury.

Laybourne, Keith (1993) 'The Guild of Help and the Changing Face of Edwardian Philanthropy', *Urban History*, **20**, (1).

Leach, P.A. (1910) 'Guilds of Help and Charitable Agencies in Relation to Statutory Poor Relief', *Proceedings of the 22nd Annual Poor Law Conference of the North Midland Districts*, 1910, London: P.S. King.

Le Grand, Julian (1991) 'Quasi-markets and Social Policy', *The Economic Journal*, **101**, September.

Le Grand, Julian (1993) *Quasi-markets and Community Care*, Bristol: School for Advanced Urban Studies.

Leira, A. (1992) *Welfare States and Working Mothers: The Scandinavian Experience*, Cambridge: Cambridge University Press.

Lewis, Jane (1982) 'Parents, Children, School Fees and the London School Board, 1870–1890', *History of Education*, **11**, (4).

Lewis, Jane (1986) *What Price Community Medicine?*, Brighton: Wheatsheaf.

Lewis, Jane (1993) 'Developing the Mixed Economy of Care: Emerging Issues for Voluntary Organisations', *Journal of Social Policy*, **22**, (2).

Lewis, Jane (1994) 'Voluntary Organisations in "New Partnership" with Local Authorities: The Anatomy of a Contract', *Social Policy and Administration*, **28**, (3).

Lewis, Jane and Brookes, Barbara (1983) 'A Reassessment of the Work of the Peckham Health Centre, 1926–1951', *Milbank Memorial Fund Quarterly/Health and Society*, **61**, (2).

Lewis, Jane, Clark, David and Morgan, David (1992) *Whom God Hath Joined Together. The Work of Marriage Guidance*, London: Routledge.

Lindsay, A.D. (1945) 'Conclusion' in A.F.C. Bourdillon (ed.), *Voluntary Social Services. Their Place in the Modern State*, London: Methuen.

Llewellyn Smith, H. (1937) *The Borderland between Public and Voluntary Action in the Social Services*, Sidney Ball Lecture, London: Oxford University Press.

Loch, C.S. (1885) *A New Chapter in Charity Organisation. Private Memorandum for the COS*, London: COS.

Loch, C.S. (1892) *Charity Organisation*, London: Swan Sonnenschein. (First edition 1890.)

Loch, C.S. (1893) *Charity Organisation*, Occasional Paper, no. 40, London: COS.

Loch, C.S. (1895) 'Canon Barnett and the Charity Organisation Society', *Charity Organisation Review*, August.

Loch, C.S. (1903) *The Future of Local Charity Organisation*, Private and Confidential Memorandum to members of the COS, London: COS.

Loch, C.S. (1904) *Methods of Social Advance*, London: Macmillan.

Loch, C.S. (1910) '"A Social Democracy" and "Social Welfare"', *Charity Organisation Review*, June.

Loch, C.S. (1916) 'The Programme of Charity Organisation', *Charity Organisation Review*, July.

Loch, C.S. (1923) *A Great Ideal and its Champion. Papers and Addresses by the late Sir C. S. Loch*, London: Allen and Unwin.

Lowe, R. (1993) *The Welfare State in Britain since 1945*, London: Macmillan

Macadam, E. (1934) *The New Philanthropy. A Study of the Relations between the Statutory and Voluntary Social Services*, London: George Allen and Unwin.

McBriar, A.M. (1987) *An Edwardian Mixed Doubles: The Bosanquets versus the Webbs. A Study in British Policy, 1890–1929*, Oxford: Clarendon Press.

McDougall, Kay and Cormack, Una (1954) 'Casework in Practice', in C. Morris (ed.), *Social Casework in Great Britain*, London: Allen and Unwin.

Mace, David R. (1945) *The Outlook for Marriage*, London: Marriage Guidance Committee.

Mace, David R. (1948) *Marriage Crisis*, London: Delisle.

MacIver, R.M. (1931) *The Contribution of Sociology to Social Work*, New York: Columbia University Press.

Mackay, T. (1889) *The English Poor*, London: John Murray.

Mackay, T. (1896) *Methods of Social Reform*, London: John Murray.

Mackay, T. (1913) *The Dangers of Democracy*, London: John Murray.

McKibbin, Ross (1978) 'Social Class and Social Observation in Edwardian England', *Transactions of the Royal Historical Society*, **28**.

MacKinnon, Mary (1987) 'English Poor Law Policy and the Crusade against Outrelief', *Journal of Economic History*, **XLVII**.

Marchant, James (ed.) (1946) *Rebuilding Family Life in the Post War World*, London: Odhams.

Marks, Lara (1992) 'Safeguarding the Health of the Community: Maternal and Infant Welfare Services in four London Boroughs, 1902–1936', paper given at the Society for the Social History of Medicine Annual Conference, 3–5 July.

Marshall, A. (1892) 'Poor-Law Reform', *The Economic Journal*, **2**, (6).

Marshall, A. and Marshall, M. (1879) *The Economics of Industry*, London: Macmillan.

Masterman, N. (1995) 'The COS of the Future', *Charity Organisation Review*, June.

Masterman, N. (1906) 'The Guild of Help Movement', *Charity Organisation Review*, September.

Maurice, C. Edmund (1913) *Life of Octavia Hill*, London: Macmillan.

Maurice, Emily (ed.) (1928) *Octavia Hill: Early Ideals*, London: Allen and Unwin.

Mayer, John E. and Timms, Noel (1970) *The Client Speaks. Working Class Impressions of Casework*, London: Routledge and Kegan Paul.

Mess, H.A. (1947) *Voluntary Services since 1918*, London: Kegan Paul, Trench & Trubner.

Milford Conference (1929) *Social Casework: Generic and Specific. An Outline. A Report of the Milford Conference. Studies in the Practice of Social Work*, no. 2, New York: American Association of Social Workers.

Milledge, W. (1906) 'Guilds of Help', *Charity Organisation Review*, July.

Ministry of Education (1955) *Report of the Committee on Maladjusted Children*, London: HMSO.

Ministry of Health and Department of Health for Scotland (1959) *Report of the Working Party on Social Workers in the Local Authority Health and Welfare Services*, London: HMSO.

Moore, G.E. (1968) *Principia Ethica*, Cambridge: Cambridge University Press. (First edition 1903.)

Morris, Cherry (ed.) (1954) *Social Casework in Great Britain*, 2nd edn, London: Faber and Faber.

Morris, Parker (1927) 'The Respective Spheres of Public Authorities and Voluntary Organisations in the Administration of Social Services', *Public Administration*, **5**, (4).

National Institute of Social Work (1982) *Social Workers: their Role and Tasks*, London: Bedford Square Press.

NCVO (National Council of Voluntary Organisations) (1990) *Working Party Report on Effectiveness and the Voluntary Sector*, London: NCVO.

*NCVO News* (1993) 'The Ups and Downs of Local Funding', no. 47, September.

Osborn, C. (1910) 'The Guild of Help Movement', *Charity Organisation Review*, June.

Owen, D. (1965) *English Philanthropy 1660–1960*, Cambridge, Mass.: Belknap Press of Harvard University Press.

Parsloe, Phyllida (1981) *Social Services Area Teams*, London: Allen and Unwins.

Parsons, R. and Bales, R.F. (1955) *Family Socialization and Interaction Process*, Glencoe, Ill.: Free Press.

Pearse, Innes and Crocker, Lucy H. (1943) *The Peckham Experiment. A Study in the Living Structure of Society*, London: Allen and Unwin.

Perlman, Helen Harris (ed.) (1969) *Helping. Charlotte Towle on Social Work and Social Casework*, Chicago: University of Chicago Press.

Perlman, Helen Harris (1970) 'The Problem-Solving Model in Social Casework', in R.W. Roberts and R.H. Nee (eds), *Theories of Social Casework*, Chicago: University of Chicago Press.

Philp, A.F. and Timms Noel (1957) *The Problem of 'the Problem Family'. A Critical Review of the literature concerning the 'Problem Family' and its Treatment*, London: Family Service Units.

Pincus, Lily (ed.) (1962) *The Marital Relationship as a Focus for Casework*, London: Institute for Marital Studies.

Pinker, R.A. (1990) *Social Work in an Enterprise Society*, London: Routledge.

Pollitt, Christopher (1993) *Managerialism and the Public Services*, 2nd edn, Oxford: Blackwell.

Pringle, Rev. J.C. (1927) 'Charity Organisation, Science and Politics', *Charity Organisation Quarterly*, July.

Pringle, Rev. J.C. (1933) *British Social Services. The Nation's Appeal to the Housewife and her Response*, London: Longmans.

Pringle, Rev. J.C. (1937) *Social Work of the London Churches. Being some account of the Metropolitan Visiting and Relief Association 1843–1937*, London: Oxford University Press.

Pringle, Rev. J.C. (1938) 'Community Effects to be sought in the process of performing Primary Human Duties', *Report of the Third International Conference on Social Work*, London: Le Play House Press.

Prochaska, F. (1988) *The Voluntary Impulse. Philanthropy in Modern Britain*, London: Faber and Faber.

Quinn, R.E. and Cameron, K. (1983) 'Organizational Life cycles and Shifting Criteria of Effectiveness: Some Preliminary Evidence', *Management Science*, **29**, (1).

Rein, Martin (1970) 'The Cross-Roads for Social Work', *Social Work*, **27**, October.

Richmond, Mary (1899) *Friendly Visiting among the Poor. A Handbook for Charity Workers*, New York: Macmillan.

Richmond, Mary (1917) *Social Diagnosis*, New York: Russell Sage Foundation.

Richmond, Mary (1930) *The Long View. Papers and Addresses by Mary E. Richmond, selected and edited by Joanna C. Colcord*, New York: Russell Sage Foundation.

Robinson, Virginia P. (1930) *A Changing Psychology in Social Case Work*, Chapel Hill: University of North Carolina Press.

Rodgers, Barbara N. and Dixon, Julia (1960) *Portrait of Social Work. A Study of Social Services in a Northern Town*, Oxford: Oxford University Press.

Rooff, M.( 1972) *A Hundred Years of Family Welfare*, London: Michael Joseph.

Rose, M. (1981) 'The Crisis of Poor Relief in England, 1860–1890', in W.J. Mommse (ed.), *The Emergence of the Welfare State in Britain and Germany*, London: Croom Helm.

Rose, M. (1988) 'The Disappearing Pauper: Victorian Attitudes to the Relief of the Poor', in Eric M. Sigsworth (ed.), *In Search of Victorian Values*, Manchester: Manchester University Press.

Rose, N. (1985) *The Psychological Complex. Psychology, Politics and Society in England, 1869–1939*, London: Routledge and Kegan Paul.

Rothman, Gerald C. (1985) *Philanthropists, Therapists and Activists*, Cambridge, Mass.: Schenkman Pub. Co. Inc.

Rubinstein, D. (1969) *School Attendance in London, 1870–1906. A Social History*, Occasional Papers in Social History, no. 1, Hull: Hull University.

Russell, Bertrand (1916) *Principles of Social Reconstruction*, London: Allen and Unwin.

Sainsbury, Eric (1975) *Social Work with Families*, London: Routledge and Kegan Paul.

Salamon, L.M. (1987) 'Partners in Public Service: The Scope and Theory of Government – Nonprofit Relations', in W.W. Powell (ed.), *The Non-Profit Sector. A Research Handbook*, New Haven: Yale University Press.

Salamon, L.M. (1990) 'The Non-Profit Sector and Government in the US', in H.K. Anheier and W. Seibel (eds) *The Third Sector Comparative Studies of Nonprofit Organizations*, New York: de Guyter.

Savage, S.W. (1946) 'Intelligence and Infant Mortality in Problem Families', *British Medical Journal*, **1**.

Saxon-Harrold, S. (1990) 'Competition, Resources and Strategy in the British Non-Profit Sector', in H.K. Anheier and W. Siebel (eds.) *The Third Sector Comparative Studies of Nonprofit Organisations*, New York: de Gruyter.

Shairp, L.V. (1912) 'The COS and the Guilds of Help', *Charity Organisation Review*, July.

Sherrington, Christine (1985) 'The NSPCC in Transition, 1884–1983. A Study of Organizational Survival', unpublished PhD, University of London.

Simey, T.S. (1937) *Principles of Social Administration*, Oxford: Oxford University Press.

Simey, T.S. (1956–7) 'Social Service as a Profession', *Social Service Quarterly*, **XXX**, (3).

Smith, Winifred P. and Bate, Helen A. (1951) *Family Casework and the Country Dweller*, London: FWA.

Spence, J.C. (1946) 'The Purpose of the Family', Convocation Lecture for the National Children's Home, London.

Stedman Jones, Gareth (1976) *Outcast London*, Harmondsworth: Penguin.

Stephens, Tom (ed.) (1946) *Problem Families. An Experiment in Social Rehabilitation*, London: Victor Gollancz.

Stevenson, O. (1968) 'The Seebohm Report and Social Work Education', *Social Work*, **25**, October.

Stevenson, O. and Parsloe, P. (1978) *Social Services Teams: The Practitioners' View*, London: HMSO.

Sutherland, J.D. (1957) 'Casework in a Community Setting', *Social Work*, **14**, January.

Sutter, Julie (1904) *Britain's Next Campaign*, London: R. Brimley Johnson. (First edition 1901.)

Sutter, Julie (1907) *Britain's Hope. An Open Letter Concerning the Pressing Social Problems to the Rt. Hon. John Burns* [President of the Local Government Board], London: James Clarke.

Taylor, M. and Hoggett, P. (1993) 'Quasi-Markets and the Transformation of the Independent Sector', paper presented at the conference on 'Quasi-Markets in Public Sector Service Delivery: the Emerging Findings', School for Advanced Urban Studies, University of Bristol, 22–4 March.

Taylor, Marilyn (1992) 'The Changing role of the Nonprofit Sector in Britain: Moving Toward the Market', in B. Gidron, R. Kramer and L.M. Salamon (eds), *Government and the Third Sector: Emerging Relationships in Welfare States*, New York: Jossey-Bass.

Tebbut, Melanie (1983) *Making Ends Meet. Pawnbroking and Working-Class Credit*, Leicester: Leicester University Press.

Thane, Pat (1978) 'Women and the Poor Law in Victorian and Edwardian England', *History Workshop Journal*, no. 6, Autumn.

Thane, Pat (1990) 'Government and Society in England and Wales, 1750–1914', in F.M.L. Thompson (ed.) *The Cambridge Social History of Britain, 1750–1950*, vol. 3, *Social Agencies and Institutions*, Cambridge: Cambridge University Press.

Thane, Pat (1993) 'Women in the British Labour Party and the Construction of State Welfare', in Seth Koven and Sonya Michel (eds), *Mothers of a New World. Maternalist Politics and the Origins of Welfare States*, London: Routledge.

Thom, Deborah (1992) 'Wishes, Anxieties, Play and Gestures: Child Guidance in Inter-War England', in Roger Cooter (ed.), *In the Name of the Child. Health and Welfare, 1880–1940*, London: Routledge.

Thomas, A. Ernest (1933) 'Guilds of Help, their Formation and Growth', paper given to the Annual Conference of Social Service and Guilds of Help, NCVO Library.

Thomson, M. (1992) 'The Problem of Mental Deficiency in England and Wales, c. 1913–1946', unpublished DPhil., Oxford University.

Timms, Noel (1962) 'The Public and the Social Worker', *Social Work*, **19**, January.

Timms, Noel (1964) *Psychiatric Social Work in Great Britain 1939–1962*, London: Routledge and Kegan Paul.

Titmuss, R.M. (1954) 'The Administrative Setting of Social Service', *Case Conference*, **1**, (1), 5–11.

Titmuss, R.M. (1974) *Social Policy*, London: Allen and Unwin.

Towle, Charlotte (1945) *Common Human Needs*, London: Allen and Unwin.

Towle, Charlotte (1956) *Some Reflections on Social Work Education*, London: FWA.

Townshend, Mrs (1911) 'The Case against the COS', Fabian Tract no. 158.

Urwick, E.J. (1903) 'Social Education of Yesterday and Tomorrow', *Charity Organisation Review*, November.

Urwick, E.J. (1912) *A Philosophy of Social Progress*, London: Methuen.

Urwick, E.J. (1930) *The Principle of Reciprocity in Social Life and Action*, Second Charles Loch Memorial Lecture, London: COS.

Urwin, Cathy and Sharland, Elaine (1992) 'From Bodies to Minds in Childcare Literature. Advice to Parents in Inter-War Britain', in Roger Cooter (ed.), *In the Name of the Child. Health and Welfare 1880–1940*, London: Routledge.

Utting, W.B. (1978) 'Social Work and the State', Loch Memorial Lecture, London: FWA.

Utting, W.B. (1992) 'Social Work – what went wrong?', *London Review of Books*, 14 May.

Vicinus, M. (1985) *Independent Women. Work and Community for Single Women, 1850–1920*, London: Virago.

Vincent, A.W. (1984) 'The Poor Law Reports of 1909 and the Social Theory of the Charity Organisation Society', *Victorian Studies*, **27**, (3).

Vincent, A.W. (ed.) (1986) *The Philosophy of T.H. Green*, Aldershot: Gower.

Waine, Barbara (1992) 'The Voluntary Sector – the Thatcher Years', in N. Manning and R. Page (eds) *Social Policy Review*, **4**, London: Social Policy Association.

Ware, A. (1989) *Between Profit and State. Intermediate Organisations in Britain and the US*, Cambridge: Polity.

Ware, A. (1990) 'Meeting Needs through Voluntary Action: Does Market Society Corrode Altruism?', in A. Ware and R.E. Goodin (eds), *Needs and Welfare*, Sage Modern Politics Series, no. 26, London: Sage.

Ware, A. and Goodin R.E. (1990) 'Introduction', in A. Ware and R.E. Goodin (eds), *Needs and Welfare*, Sage Modern Politics Series, no. 26, London: Sage.

Webb, Beatrice (1926) *My Apprenticeship*, Cambridge: Cambridge University Press.

Webb S. and Webb, B. (1912) *The Prevention of Destitution*, London: by the authors.

Weisbrod, B.A. (1988) *The Nonprofit Economy*, Cambridge, Mass.: Harvard University Press.

Wicks, M. (1984) 'Enter Right: The Family Patrol Group', *New Society*, 24 February.

Willetts, D. (1992) *Modern Conservatism*, Harmondsworth: Penguin.

Wilson, A.T.M. (1947) 'The Development of a Scientific Basis in Family Casework', *Social Work*, **4**, July.

Wilson, Roger (1950) 'Social Work in a Changing Society', *Social Work*, **7**, October.

Wistow, G., Knapp, M., Hardy, B. and Allen, C. (1992) 'From Providing to Enabling: Local Authorities and the Mixed Economy of Social Care', *Public Administration*, **70**.

Wistow, G., Knapp, M, Hardy, B. and Allen, C. (1994) *Social Care in a Mixed Economy*, Buckingham: Open University Press.

Wofinden, R.C. (1950) *Problem Families in Bristol*, Occasional Papers in Eugenics, no. 6, London: The Eugenics Society and Cassell.

Wolfenden Committee (1978) *The Future of Voluntary Organisations*, London: Croom Helm.

Women's Group on Public Welfare (1943) *Our Towns*, Oxford: Oxford University Press.

Women's Group on Public Welfare (1948) *The Neglected Child and His Family*, Oxford: Oxford University Press.

Woodroofe, K. (1962) *From Charity to Social Work in England and the United States*, London: Routledge and Kegan Paul.

Woolcombe, H.L. (1893) *Enquiry and Office Work*, Occasional Paper, no. 54, London: COS.

Wootton, B., assisted by Seal, V.G. and Chambers, R. (1959) *Social Science and Social Pathology*, London: Allen and Unwin.

Wootton, B. (1959b) 'Daddy Knows Best', *Twentieth Century*, **CLXVI**, October.

Wootton, B. (1960) 'The Image of the Social Worker', *British Journal of Sociology*, **11**, December.

Yelloly, M. (1980) *Social Work Theory and Psychoanalysis*, New York: Van Nostrand Reinhold.

Yeo, S. (1976) *Religion and Voluntary Organisations in Crisis*, London: Croom Helm.

Younghusband, Eileen (1947) *Report on the Employment and Training of Social Workers*, Edinburgh: Carnegie UK Trust.

Younghusband, Eileen (1951) *Social Work in Britain. A Supplementary Report on the Employment and Training of Social Workers*, Edinburgh: Carnegie UK Trust.

Younghusband, Eileen (1954) 'Conclusion', in C. Morris (ed.), *Social Casework in Great Britain*, London: Allen and Unwin.

Younghusband, Eileen (1960) 'Social Work in Public and Voluntary Agencies', *Social Work*, **17**, January.

Younghusband, Eileen (1964) *Social Work and Social Change*, London: Allen and Unwin.

# Index